The Gospels for Prayer

compiled by
John C. Edwards S.J.

CATHOLIC TRUTH SOCIETY
PUBLISHERS TO THE HOLY SEE

LONDON

First published 1981 by the
Incorporated Catholic Truth Society
38–40 Eccleston Square
London SW1V 1PD

ISBN 0 85183 356 X

AC

Scripture texts are from the Catholic edition
of the Revised Standard Version of The Holy Bible

Printed by Staples Printers St Albans Limited, at The Priory Press

Contents

Introduction

'And this is eternal life, that they know thee the only true God, and Jesus Christ whom thou hast sent' (Jn 17:3).

An 'interior knowledge of our Lord', as St Ignatius calls it, is a grace, a gift to be asked for. Preparation, however, is needed to receive it. It is useful to find out, for instance, what things pleased him, what angered him; what he praised, what were his dominant thoughts.

One way of doing this is to read related texts. Even though they are disjointed the cumulative effect can lend a necessary emphasis previously unnoticed.

It is not enough to look up a scripture commentary on a word or a theme, and anyway the labour would frustrate the praying. The selection provided here, and the headings under which they appear, are obviously a personal choice. Since we are free to use scripture in any conceivable way we wish, providing we do not contradict the teaching of the Church, I make no apology for the subjective element.

This selection is made to help prayer. Specifically, retreatants making the Spiritual Exercises of St Ignatius may find it useful. An Appendix giving references to the text is provided.

John Edwards S.J.

1. Prayer

i. Jesus prays 'liturgically'

Lk. 2:43	. . . and when the feast was ended, as they were returning, the boy Jesus stayed behind in Jerusalem. His parents did not know it . . . .
Mk 1:9	In those days Jesus came from Nazareth of Galilee and was baptized by John in the Jordan.
Jn 2:13	The Passover of the Jews was at hand, and Jesus went up to Jerusalem.
Lk. 4:16	And he came to Nazareth, where he had been brought up; and he went to the synagogue, as his custom was, on the sabbath day.
Jn 5:1	After this there was a feast of the Jews, and Jesus went up to Jerusalem.
Jn 7:10	But after his brethren had gone up to the feast, then he also went up, not publicly but in private.
Jn 10:22	It was the feast of the Dedication at Jerusalem . . . .
Mk 10:32	And they were on the road, going up to Jerusalem, and Jesus was walking ahead of them; and they were amazed, and those who followed were afraid. And taking the twelve again, he began to tell them what was to happen to him . . . .
Lk. 19:28	. . . he went on ahead, going up to Jerusalem.
Lk. 22:17	And he took a cup, and when he had given thanks he said, 'Take this, and divide it among yourselves . . . .'
Mt. 26:26-28	Now as they were eating, Jesus took bread, and blessed, and broke it, and gave it to the disciples and said, 'Take, eat; this is my body.' And he took a cup, and when he had given thanks he gave it to them saying, 'Drink of it, all of you; for this is my blood of the covenant, which is poured out for many for the forgiveness of sins. . . .'
Mt. 26:30	And when they had sung a hymn, they went out to the Mount of Olives.

Lk. 24:29-31 ... but they constrained him, saying, 'Stay with us, for it is toward evening and the day is now far spent.' So he went in to stay with them. When he was at table with them, he took the bread and blessed, and broke it, and gave it to them. And their eyes were opened and they recognized him; and he vanished out of their sight.

ii. Jesus prays privately

Mk 1:12 The Spirit immediately drove him out into the wilderness.

Mk 1:35 And in the morning, a great while before day, he rose and went out to a lonely place, and there he prayed.

Lk. 5:16 But he withdrew to the wilderness and prayed.

Lk. 6:12 In these days he went out into the hills to pray; and all night he continued in prayer to God.

Mt. 14:23 And after he had dismissed the crowds he went up into the hills by himself to pray. When evening came, he was there alone ....

Lk. 9:28,29 Now about eight days after these sayings he took with him Peter and John and James, and went up on the mountain to pray. And as he was praying, the appearance of his countenance was altered, and his raiment became dazzling white.

Jn 11:33 When Jesus saw her weeping, and the Jews who came with her also weeping, he was deeply moved in spirit and troubled ....

Lk. 22:31,32 'Simon, Simon, behold, Satan demanded to have you, that he might sift you like wheat, but I have prayed for you that your faith may not fail; and when you have turned again, strengthen your brethren.'

iii. Jesus prays aloud

Mk 7:34 ... and looking up to heaven, he sighed, and said to him, 'Ephphatha,' that is, 'Be opened.'

Lk. 10:21 In that same hour he rejoiced in the Holy Spirit and said, 'I thank thee, Father, Lord of heaven and earth, that thou hast hidden these things from the wise and understanding and revealed them to babes; yea, Father, for such was thy gracious will . . . .'

Mt. 19:13,14 Then children were brought to him that he might lay his hands on them and pray. The disciples rebuked the people; but Jesus said, 'Let the children come to me, and do not hinder them; for to such belongs the kingdom of heaven.'

Mk 10:16 And he took them in his arms and blessed them, laying his hands upon them.

Jn 11:41,42 So they took away the stone. And Jesus lifted up his eyes and said, 'Father, I thank thee that thou hast heard me. I knew that thou hearest me always, but I have said this on account of the people standing by, that they may believe that thou didst send me.'

Jn 12:27 'Now is my soul troubled. And what shall I say? "Father, save me from this hour"? No, for this purpose I have come to this hour . . . .'

Jn 17:1-26 When Jesus had spoken these words, he lifted up his eyes to heaven and said, 'Father, the hour has come; glorify thy Son that the Son may glorify thee, since thou hast given him power over all flesh, to give eternal life to all whom thou hast given him. And this is eternal life, that they know thee the only true God, and Jesus Christ whom thou has sent. I glorified thee on earth having accomplished the work which thou gavest me to do; and now, Father, glorify thou me in thy own presence with the glory which I had with thee before the world was made.

'I have manifested thy name to the men whom thou gavest me out of the world; thine they were, and thou gavest them to me, and they have kept thy word. Now they know that everything that thou hast given me is from thee; for I have given them the words which thou gavest to me, and they have received them and know in truth that I came from thee; and they have believed that thou didst send me. I am praying for them; I am not praying for the world but for those whom thou hast given me, for they are thine; all mine are thine, and thine are mine, and I am glorified in them. And now I am no more in the world, but they are in the world, and I am coming to thee. Holy Father, keep them in thy name, which thou hast given me, that they may be one, even as we are one. While I was with them, I kept them in thy name, which thou hast given me; I have guarded them, and none of them is lost but the son of perdition, that the scripture might be fulfilled. But now I am coming to thee; and these things I speak in the world, that they may have my joy fulfilled in themselves. I have given them thy word; and the world has hated them because they are not of the world, even as I am not of the world. I do not pray that thou shouldst take them out of the world, but that thou shouldst keep them from the evil one. They are not of the world, even as I am not of the world. Sanctify them in the truth; thy word is truth. As thou didst send me into the world, so I have sent them into the world. And for their sake I consecrate myself, that they also may be consecrated in truth.

'I do not pray for these only, but also for those who believe in me through their word, that they may all be one; even as thou, Father, art in me, and I in thee, that they also may be in us, so that the world may believe that thou hast sent me. The glory which thou hast given me I have given to them, that they may be one even as we are one, I in them and thou in me, that they may become perfectly one, so that the world may know that thou hast sent me and hast loved them even as thou hast loved me. Father, I desire that they also, whom thou hast given me, may be with me where I am, to behold my glory which thou hast given me in thy love for me before the foundation of the world. O righteous Father, the world has not known thee, But I have known thee; and these know that thou hast sent me. I made known to them thy name, and I will make it known, that the love with which thou hast loved me may be in them, and I in them.'

Mk 14:35-36 And going a little farther, he fell on the ground and prayed that, if it were possible, the hour might pass from him. And he said, 'Abba, Father, all things are possible to thee; remove this cup from me; yet not what I will, but what thou wilt.'

Lk. 22:43-44	And there appeared to him an angel from heaven, strengthening him. And being in an agony he prayed more earnestly; and his sweat became like great drops of blood falling down upon the ground.
Mt. 26:42	Again, for the second time, he went away and prayed, 'My Father, if this cannot pass unless I drink it, thy will be done.'
Mt. 26:44	So, leaving them again, he went away and prayed for the third time, saying the same words.
Lk. 23:34	And Jesus said, 'Father, forgive them; for they know not what they do.'
Mt. 27:46	And about the ninth hour Jesus cried with a loud voice, 'Eli, Eli, lama sabachthani?' that is, 'My God, my God, why hast thou forsaken me?'
Lk. 23:46	Then Jesus, crying with a loud voice, said, 'Father, into thy hands I commit my spirit.'

iv. Jesus teaches about prayer

Jn 4:49,50	The official said to him 'Sir, come down before my child dies.' Jesus said to him, 'Go; your son will live.' The man believed the word that Jesus spoke to him and went his way.
Mt. 6:5,6	'And when you pray, you must not be like the hypocrites; for they love to stand and pray in the synagogues and at the street corners, that they may be seen by men. Truly, I say to you, they have their reward. But when you pray, go into your room and shut the door and pray to your Father who is in secret; and your Father who sees in secret will reward you.'
Mt. 9:37,38	Then he said to his disciples, 'The harvest is plentiful, but the labourers are few; pray therefore the Lord of the harvest to send out labourers into his harvest.'
Mk 9:27-29	But Jesus took him by the hand and lifted him up, and he arose. And when he had entered the house, his disciples asked him privately, 'Why could we not cast it out?' And he said to them, 'This kind cannot be driven out by anything but prayer and fasting.'

Mt. 18:19,20 'Again I say to you, if two of you agree on earth about anything they ask, it will be done for them by my Father in heaven. For where two or three are gathered in my name, there am I in the midst of them.'

Lk. 10:2 And he said to them, 'The harvest is plentiful, but the labourers are few; pray therefore the Lord of the harvest to send out labourers into his harvest.'

Lk. 10:5,6 'Whatever house you enter, first say, "Peace be to this house." And if a son of peace is there, your peace shall rest upon him; but if not, it shall return to you.'

Mt. 6:7-13 'And in praying do not heap up empty phrases as the Gentiles do; for they think that they will be heard for their many words. Do not be like them, for your Father knows what you need before you ask him. Pray then like this:

Our Father who art in heaven,
Hallowed be thy name.
Thy kingdom come,
Thy will be done, on earth as it is in heaven,
Give us this day our daily bread;
And forgive us our debts,
As we also have forgiven our debtors;
And lead us not into temptation
But deliver us from evil.'

Mk. 11:25,26 And whenever you stand praying, forgive, if you have anything against any one; so that your Father also who is in heaven may forgive you your trespasses.

Lk. 11:5-13 And he said to them, 'Which of you who has a friend will go to him at midnight and say to him, "Friend, lend me three loaves; for a friend of mine has arrived on a journey, and I have nothing to set before him;" and he will answer from within, "Do not bother me; the door is now shut and my children are with me in bed; I cannot get up and give you anything"? I tell you, though he will not get up and give him anything because he is his friend, yet because of his importunity he will rise and give him whatever he needs. And I tell you, Ask, and it will be given you; seek, and you will find; knock, and it will be opened to you.

'For every one who asks receives, and he who seeks finds, and to him who knocks it will be opened. What father among you, if his son asks for a fish, will instead of a fish give him a serpent; or if he asks for an egg, will give him a scorpion? If you then, who are evil, know how to give good gifts to your children, how much more will the heavenly Father give the Holy Spirit to those who ask him.'

Mk 13:33 'Take heed, watch and pray; for you do not know when the time will come.'

Lk. 15:18 I will rise and go to my father, and I will say to him, 'Father, I have sinned against heaven and before you . . . .'

Lk. 15:21 And the son said to him, 'Father, I have sinned against heaven and before you; I am no longer worthy to be called your son.'

Lk. 18:1-8 And he told them a parable, to the effect that they ought always to pray and not lose heart. He said, 'In a certain city there was a judge who neither feared God nor regarded man; and there was a widow in that city who kept coming to him and saying, "Vindicate me against my adversary." For a while he refused; but afterward he said to himself, "Though I neither fear God nor regard man, yet because this widow bothers me, I will vindicate her, or she will wear me out by her continual coming."' And the Lord said, 'Hear what the unrighteous judge says. And will not God vindicate his elect, who cry to him day and night? I tell you, he will vindicate them speedily. Nevertheless, when the Son of man comes, will he find faith on earth?'

Lk. 18:13,14 'But the tax collector, standing far off, would not even lift up his eyes to heaven, but beat his breast, saying, "God, be merciful to me a sinner." I tell you, this man went down to his house justified rather than the other; for every one who exalts himself will be humbled, but he who humbles himself will be exalted.'

Mk 11:22-25 And Jesus answered them, 'Have faith in God. Truly, I say to you, whoever says to this mountain, "Be taken up and cast into the sea," and does not doubt in his heart, but believes that what he says will come to pass, it will be done for him. Therefore I tell you, whatever you ask in prayer, believe that you receive it, and you will. And whenever you stand praying, forgive, if you have anything against any one; so that your Father also who is in heaven may forgive you your trespasses.'

Mt. 21:22 'And whatever you ask in prayer, you will receive, if you have faith.'

Lk. 21:36 'But watch at all times, praying that you may have strength to escape all these things that will take place, and to stand before the Son of man.'

Jn 16:23-27 'In that day you will ask nothing of me. Truly, truly, I say to you, if you ask anything of the Father, he will give it to you in my name. Hitherto you have asked nothing in my name; ask, and you will receive, that your joy may be full.

'I have said this to you in figures; the hour is coming when I shall no longer speak to you in figures but tell you plainly of the Father. In that day you will ask in my name; and I do not say to you that I shall pray the Father for you; for the Father himself loves you, because you have loved me and have believed that I came from the Father.'

Jn 14:12-14 'Truly, truly, I say to you, he who believes in me will also do the works that I do; and greater works than these will he do, because I go to the Father. Whatever you ask in my name, I will do it, that the Father may be glorified in the Son; if you ask anything in my name, I will do it.'

Jn 15:7 'If you abide in me, and my words abide in you, ask whatever you will, and it shall be done for you.'

Jn 15:16 '... I chose and appointed you that you should go and bear fruit and that your fruit should abide; so that whatever you ask the Father in my name, he may give it to you.'

Jn 15:18 'If the world hates you, know that it has hated me before it hated you.'

Jn 16:13 'When the Spirit of Truth comes, he will guide you into all truth; for he will not speak on his own authority, but whatever he hears he will speak. . . .'

Lk. 22:40 And when he came to the place he said to them, 'Pray that you may not enter into temptation.'

Lk. 22:46 . . . And he said to them, 'Why do you sleep,? Rise and pray that you may not enter into temptation.'

Mt. 26:41 'Watch and pray that you may not enter into temptation; the spirit indeed is willing, but the flesh is weak.'

v. Jesus' mother and friends pray

Lk. 1:8-10 Now while he was serving as priest before God when his division was on duty, according to the custom of the priesthood, it fell to him by lot to enter the temple of the Lord and burn incense. And the whole multitude of the people were praying outside at the hour of incense.

Lk. 1:46-55 And Mary said,
'My soul magnifies the Lord, and my spirit rejoices in God my Saviour,
for he has regarded the low estate of his handmaiden.
For behold, henceforth all generations will call me blessed;
for he who is mighty has done great things for me, and holy is his name.
And his mercy is on those who fear him from generation to generation.
He has shown strength with his arm,
he has scattered the proud in the imagination of their hearts.
he has put down the mighty from their thrones,
and exalted those of low degree;
he has filled the hungry with good things,
and the rich he has sent empty away.
He has helped his servant Israel, in remembrance of his mercy,
as he spoke to our fathers,
To Abraham and to his posterity for ever.'

Lk. 1:67-79 . . . Zechariah was filled with the Holy Spirit, and prophesied, saying,
'Blessed be the Lord God of Israel, for he has visited and redeemed his people,

and has raised up a horn of salvation for us
in the house of his servant David,
as he spoke by the mouth of his holy prophets from of old,
that we should be saved from our enemies,
and from the hand of all who hate us;
to perform the mercy promised to our fathers,
and to remember his holy covenant,
the oath which he swore to our father Abraham, to grant us
that we, being delivered from the hand of our enemies,
might serve him without fear,
in holiness and righteousness before him all the days of our life.
And you, child, will be called the prophet of the Most High;
for you will go before the Lord to prepare his ways,
to give knowledge of salvation to his people
in the forgiveness of their sins,
through the tender mercy of our God,
when the day shall dawn upon us from on high
to give light to those who sit in darkness and in the shadow of death,
to guide our feet into the way of peace.'

Lk. 2:13,14 And suddenly there was with the angel a multitude of the heavenly host praising God and saying, 'Glory to God in the highest, and on earth peace among men with whom he is pleased.'

Lk. 2:19,20 But Mary kept all these things, pondering them in her heart. And the shepherds returned, glorifying and praising God for all they had heard and seen, as it had been told them.

Lk. 2:22,23 And when the time came for the purification according to the law of Moses, they brought him up to Jerusalem to present him to the Lord (as it is written in the law of the Lord 'Every male that opens the womb shall be called holy to the Lord').

Lk. 2:27-33 And inspired by the Spirit he came into the temple; and when the parents brought in the child Jesus, to do for him according to the custom of the law, he took him up in his arms and blessed God and said,

'Lord, now lettest thou thy servant depart in peace,
according to thy word;
for mine eyes have seen thy salvation
which thou hast prepared in the presence of all peoples,
a light for revelation to the Gentiles,
and for glory to thy people Israel.'

And his father and his mother marvelled at what was said about him . . . .

Lk. 2:37,38 She did not depart from the temple, worshipping with fasting and prayer night and day. And coming up at that very hour she gave thanks to God, and spoke of him to all who were looking for the redemption of Jerusalem.

Mt. 2:11 . . . and going into the house they saw the child with Mary his mother, and they fell down and worshipped him. Then, opening their treasures, they offered him gifts, gold and frankincense and myrrh.

Lk. 2:41 Now his parents went to Jerusalem every year at the feast of the Passover.

Lk. 2:51 And he went down with them and came to Nazareth and was obedient to them; and his mother kept all these things in her heart.

Mt. 4:11 Then the devil left him, and behold, angels came and ministered to him.

Lk. 7:4,5 And when they came to Jesus, they besought him earnestly, saying, 'He is worthy to have you do this for him, for he loves our nation, and he built us our synagogue.'

Mt. 8:8,9 But the centurion answered him, 'Lord, I am not worthy to have you come under my roof; but only say the word, and my servant will be healed. For I am a man under authority, with soldiers under me; and I say to one, "Go," and he goes, and to another, "Come," and he comes, and to my slave, "Do this," and he does it.'

Mt. 9:8 When the crowds saw it, they were afraid, and they glorified God, who had given such authority to men.

Mk 9:23,24	And Jesus said to him, 'If you can. All things are possible to him who believes.' Immediately the father of the child cried out and said, 'I believe; help my unbelief.'
Mt. 9:27	And as Jesus passed on from there, two blind men followed him, crying aloud, 'Have mercy on us, Son of David.'
Mt. 14:28-30	And Peter answered him, 'Lord, if it is you, bid me come to you on the water.' He said, 'Come.' So Peter got out of the boat and walked on the water and came to Jesus; but when he saw the wind, he was afraid, and beginning to sink he cried out, 'Lord, save me.'
Mt. 14:33	And those in the boat worshipped him, saying, 'Truly you are the Son of God.'
Mt. 15:22-5	And behold, a Canaanite woman from that region came out and cried, 'Have mercy on me, O Lord, Son of David; my daughter is severely possessed by a demon.' But he did not answer her a word. And his disciples came and begged him, saying, 'Send her away, for she is crying after us.' He answered, 'I was sent only to the lost sheep of the house of Israel.' But she came and knelt before him saying, 'Lord, help me.'
Jn 9:38	He said, 'Lord, I believe'; and he worshipped him.
Lk. 17:13	. . . and lifted up their voices and said, 'Jesus, Master, have mercy on us.'
Lk. 17:15,16	Then one of them, when he saw that he was healed, turned back, praising God with a loud voice; and he fell on his face at Jesus' feet, giving him thanks.
Jn 11:21,22	Martha said to Jesus, 'Lord, if you had been here, my brother would not have died. And even now I know that whatever you ask from God, God will give you.'
Mk 10:35	And James and John, the sons of Zebedee, came forward to him, and said to him, 'Teacher, we want you to do for us whatever we ask of you.'
Mk 10:47,48	And when he heard that it was Jesus of Nazareth, he began to cry out and say, 'Jesus, Son of David, have

mercy on me.' And many rebuked him, telling him to be silent; but he cried out all the more, 'Son of David, have mercy on me.'

Lk. 18:41-43 'What do you want me to do for you?' He said, 'Lord, let me receive my sight.' And Jesus said to him, 'Receive your sight; your faith has made you well.' And immediately he received his sight and followed him, glorifying God; and all the people, when they saw it, gave praise to God.

Mt. 21:9 And the crowds that went before him and that followed him shouted, 'Hosanna to the Son of David. Blessed is he who comes in the name of the Lord. Hosanna in the highest.'

Lk. 23:42 And he said, 'Jesus remember me when you come in your kingly power.'

Lk. 23:47 Now when the centurion saw what had taken place, he praised God, and said, 'Certainly this man was innocent.'

Jn 20:16 Jesus said to her, 'Mary.' She turned and said to him in Hebrew, 'Rabboni!' (which means Teacher).

Jn 20:27,28 Then he said to Thomas, 'Put your finger here and see my hands; and put out your hand, and place it in my side; do not be faithless, but believing.' Thomas answered him, 'My Lord and my God.'

Jn 21:15-17 When they had finished breakfast, Jesus said to Simon Peter, 'Simon, son of John, do you love me more than these?' He said to him, 'Yes, Lord; you know that I love you.' He said to him, 'Feed my lambs.' A second time he said to him, 'Simon, son of John, do you love me?' He said to him, 'Yes, Lord; you know that I love you.' He said to him, 'Tend my sheep.' He said to him the third time, 'Simon, son of John, do you love me?' Peter was grieved because he said to him the third time, 'Do you love me?' And he said to him, 'Lord, you know everything; you know that I love you.' Jesus said to him, 'Feed my sheep.'

Lk. 24:52,53 And they worshipped him, and returned to Jerusalem with great joy, and were continually in the temple blessing God.

vi. Austerity

See also 15, 'Poverty and Self-Emptying'

Lk. 1:15	'. . . for he will be great before the Lord, and he shall drink no wine nor strong drink, and he will be filled with the Holy Spirit, even from his mother's womb.'
Lk. 2:37	She did not depart from the temple, worshipping with fasting and prayer night and day.
Mk 1:6	Now John was clothed with camel's hair, and had a leather girdle around his waist, and ate locusts and wild honey.
Mk 1:13	And he was in the wilderness forty days, tempted by Satan; and he was with the wild beasts; and the angels ministered to him.
Mk 2:18-20	Now John's disciples and the pharisees were fasting; and people came and said to him, 'Why do John's disciples and the disciples of the Pharisees fast, but your disciples do not fast?' And Jesus said to them, 'Can the wedding guests fast while the bridegroom is with them? As long as they have the bridegroom with them, they cannot fast. The days will come, when the bridegroom is taken away from them, and then they will fast in that day.'
Lk. 6:12	In those days he went out into the hills to pray; and all night he continued in prayer to God.
Mt. 5:17	'Think not that I have come to abolish the law and the prophets; I have come not to abolish them but to fulfil them.'
Mt. 5:20	'For I tell you, unless your righteousness exceeds that of the scribes and Pharisees, you will never enter the kingdom of heaven.'
Mt. 6:16-18	'And when you fast, do not look dismal, like the hypocrites, for they disfigure their faces that their fasting may be seen by men. Truly, I say to you, they have their reward. But when you fast, anoint your head and wash your face, that your fasting may not be seen by men but by your Father who is in secret; and your Father who sees in secret will reward you.'

Mt. 11:8	'Why then did you get out? To see a man clothed in soft raiment? Behold, those who wear soft raiment are in kings' houses.'
Lk. 8:14	'And as for what fell among thorns, they are those who hear, but as they go on their way they are choked by the cares and riches and pleasures of life, and their fruit does not mature.'
Mk 6:31	And he said to them 'Come away by yourselves to a lonely place, and rest a while.' For many were coming and going, and they had no leisure even to eat.
Lk. 9:23	And he said to all, 'If any man would come after me, let him deny himself and take up his cross daily and follow me.'
Mk 9:27, 28,29	But Jesus took him by the hand and lifted him up, and he arose. And when he had entered the house, his disciples asked him privately, 'Why could we not cast it out?' And he said to them, 'This kind cannot be driven out by anything but prayer and fasting.'
Mt. 18:8,9	'And if your hand or your foot causes you to sin, cut it off and throw it from you; it is better for you to enter life maimed or lame than with two hands or two feet to be thrown into the eternal fire. And if your eye causes you to sin, pluck it out and throw it from you; it is better for you to enter life with one eye than with two eyes to be thrown into the hell of fire.'
Mt. 11:21	'Woe to you, Chorazin. Woe to you, Bethsaida. For if the mighty works done in you had been done in Tyre and Sidon, they would have repented long ago in sackcloth and ashes.'
Lk. 9:58	And Jesus said to him, 'Foxes have holes, and birds of the air have nests; but the Son of man has nowhere to lay his head.'
Lk. 14:26,27	'If any man comes to me and does not hate his own father and mother and wife and children and brothers and sisters, yes, and even his own life, he cannot be my disciple. Whoever does not bear his own cross and come after me, cannot be my disciple.'

Lk. 18:28	And Peter said, 'Lo, we have left our homes and followed you.'
Lk. 24:27	And beginning with Moses and all the prophets, he interpreted to them in all the scriptures the things concerning himself.

2. Our Enemy

i. His character and style

Mt. 4:1	Then Jesus was led up by the Spirit into the wilderness to be tempted by the devil.
Mt. 4:3	And the tempter came and said to him, 'If you are the Son of God, command these stones to become loaves of bread.'
Mt. 4:5	Then the devil took him to the holy city, and set him on the pinnacle of the temple.
Mt. 4:8,9	Again, the devil took him to a very high mountain, and showed him all the kingdoms of the world and the glory of them; and he said to him, 'All these I will give you, if you will fall down and worship me.'
Lk. 4:13	And when the devil had ended every temptation, he departed from him until an opportune time.
Mk 1:23,24	And immediately there was in their synagogue, a man with an unclean spirit; and he cried out, 'What have you to do with us, Jesus of Nazareth? Have you come to destroy us? I know who you are, the Holy One of God.'
Lk. 8:12	'The ones along the path are those who have heard; then the devil comes and takes away the word from their hearts, that they may not believe and be saved.'
Mt. 13:25	'... but while men were sleeping, his enemy came and sowed weeds among the wheat, and went away.'
Mt. 13:28	He said to them 'An enemy has done this.' The servants said to him, 'Then do you want us to go and gather them?'
Mk 5:2-13	And when he had come out of the boat, there met him out of the tombs a man with an unclean spirit, who lived among the tombs; and no one could bind him any more, even with a chain; for he had often been bound with fetters and chains, but the chains he wrenched apart, and the fetters he broke in pieces; and no one had the strength to subdue him. Night and day among the tombs and on the mountains he was always crying out, and bruising himself with stones. And when he saw Jesus from afar, he ran and worshipped him; and crying out

with a loud voice, he said, 'What have you to do with me, Jesus, Son of the Most High God? I adjure you by God, do not torment me.' For he had said to him, 'Come out of the man, you unclean spirit.' And Jesus asked him, 'What is your name?' He replied, 'My name is Legion; for we are many.' And he begged him eagerly not to send them out of the country. Now a great herd of swine was feeding there on the hillside; and they begged him 'Send us to the swine; let us enter them.' So he gave them leave. And the unclean spirits came out, and entered the swine; and the herd, numbering about two thousand, rushed down the steep bank into the sea, and were drowned in the sea.

Lk. 9:39 '. . . and behold, a spirit seizes him and he suddenly cries out; it convulses him till he foams, and shatters him and will hardly leave him.'

Lk. 11:24-26 'When the unclean spirit has gone out of a man, he passes through water-less places seeking rest; and finding none he says, "I will return to my house from which I came." And when he comes he finds it swept and put in order. Then he goes and brings seven other spirits more evil than himself, and they enter and dwell there; and the last state of that man becomes worse than the first.'

Lk. 12:4,5 'I tell you, my friends, do not fear those who kill the body, and after that have no more that they can do. But I will warn you whom to fear: fear him who, after he has killed, has power to cast into hell; yes, I tell you, fear him!'

Lk. 13:16 'And ought not this woman, a daughter of Abraham whom Satan bound for eighteen years, be loosed from this bond on the sabbath day?'

Mt. 25:41 Then he will say to those at his left hand, 'Depart from me, you cursed, into the eternal fire prepared for the devil and his angels;'

Lk. 22:3 Then Satan entered into Judas called Iscariot, who was of the number of the twelve;

Jn 13:2 And during supper, when the devil had already put it into the heart of Judas Iscariot, Simon's son, to betray him . . . .

Jn 13:27 Then after the morsel, Satan entered into him. Jesus said to him, 'What you are going to do, do quickly.'

Lk. 22:31,32 'Simon, Simon, behold Satan demanded to have you, that he might sift you like wheat, but I have prayed for you that your faith may not fail; and when you have turned again, strengthen your brethren.'

Jn 14:30 'I will no longer talk much with you, for the ruler of this world is coming. He has no power over me . . . .'

Jn 15:18 'If the world hates you, know that it has hated me before it hated you.

Jn 16:11 '. . . of judgment, because the ruler of this world is judged.'

Lk. 22:53 'When I was with you day after day in the temple, you did not lay hands on me. But this is your hour, and the power of darkness.'

ii. Jesus combats him – in general

Lk. 1:51,52 'He has shown strength with his arm,
he has scattered the proud in the imagination of their hearts,
he has put down the mighty from their thrones,
and exalted those of low degree . . . .'

Lk. 1:71,74 '. . . that we should be saved from our enemies,
and from the hand of all who hate us;
to grant us that we, being delivered from the hand of our enemies,
might serve him without fear . . . .'

Mt. 4:10 Then Jesus said to him, 'Begone Satan! for it is written, "You shall worship the Lord your God and him only shall you serve." '

Mk 9:27-29 But Jesus took him by the hand and lifted him up, and he arose. And when he had entered the house, his disciples asked him privately, 'Why could we not cast it out?' And he said to them, 'This kind cannot be driven out by anything but prayer and fasting.'

Lk. 10:17-20 The seventy returned with joy, saying, 'Lord, even the demons are subject to us in your name.' And he said to them, 'I saw Satan fall like lightning from heaven.

Behold, I have given you authority to tread upon serpents and scorpions, and over all the power of the enemy; and nothing shall hurt you. Nevertheless, do not rejoice in this, that the spirits are subject to you; but rejoice that your names are written in heaven.'

Mk 3:23,24 And he called them to him, and said to them in parables, 'How can Satan cast out Satan? If a kingdom is divided against itself, that kingdom cannot stand.'

Mt. 6:13 'And lead us not into temptation,
but deliver us from evil.'

Mt. 12:28 'But if it is by the spirit of God that I cast out demons, then the kingdom of God has come upon you.'

Jn 12:31 'Now is the judgment of this world, now shall the ruler of this world be cast out . . . .'

iii. Jesus combats him – in particular

Mk 1:25-27 But Jesus rebuked him saying, 'Be silent, and come out of him.' And the unclean spirit, convulsing him and crying with a loud voice, came out of him. And they were all amazed, so that they questioned among themselves, saying, 'What is this? A new teaching! With authority he commands even the unclean spirits, and they obey him.'

Mk 1:39 And he went throughout all Galilee, preaching in their synagogues and casting out demons.

Mt. 8:16 That evening they brought to him many who were possessed with demons; and he cast out the spirits with a word, and healed all who were sick.

Mk 3:14,15 And he appointed twelve, to be with him, and to be sent out to preach, and have authority to cast out demons:

Lk. 6:18 . . . and those who were troubled with unclean spirits were cured.

Lk. 7:21 In that hour he cured many of diseases and plagues and evil spirits, and on many that were blind he bestowed sight.

Lk. 8:2 . . . and also some women who had been healed of evil spirits and infirmities: Mary, called Magdalene, from whom seven demons had gone out . . . .

Lk. 8:33	Then the demons came out of the man and entered the swine, and the herd rushed down the steep bank into the lake and were drowned.
Mk 6:7	And he called to him the twelve, and began to send them out two by two, and gave them authority over the unclean spirits.
Mk 6:13	And they cast out many demons, and anointed with oil many that were sick and healed them.
Mk 7:29	And he said to her, 'For this saying you may go your way; the demon has left your daughter.'
Mk 9:24-29	Immediately the father of the child cried out and said, 'I believe; help my unbelief.' And when Jesus saw that a crowd came running together, he rebuked the unclean spirit, saying to it, 'You dumb and deaf spirit, I command you to come out of him, and never enter him again.' And after crying out and convulsing him terribly, it came out, and the boy was like a corpse; so that most of them said, 'He is dead.' But Jesus took him by the hand and lifted him up, and he arose. And when he had entered the house, his disciples asked him privately, 'Why could we not cast it out?' And he said to them, 'This kind cannot be driven out by anything but prayer and fasting.'
Lk. 9:49,50	John answered, 'Master, we saw a man casting out demons in your name, and we forbade him, because he does not follow with us.' But Jesus said to him. 'Do not forbid him; for he that is not against you is for you.'
Lk. 10:17	The seventy returned with joy, saying, 'Lord, even the demons are subject to us in your name.'
Mt. 9:33	And when the demon had been cast out, the dumb man spoke; and the crowds marvelled, saying, 'Never was anything like this seen in Israel.'
Lk. 11:14	Now he was casting out a demon that was dumb; when the demon had gone out, the dumb man spoke, and the people marvelled,
Lk. 13:11,12	And there was a woman who had had a spirit of infirmity for eighteen years; she was bent over and could not fully straighten herself. And when Jesus saw her, he called her

and said to her, 'Woman, you are freed from your infirmity.'

Mk 16:17 — 'And these signs will accompany those who believe: in my name they will cast out demons . . . .'

iv. Men can be like the enemy of Jesus

Mt. 2:8 — . . . and he sent them to Bethlehem, saying, 'Go and search diligently for the child, and when you have found him bring me word, that I too may come and worship him.'

Mt. 2:16 — Then Herod, when he saw he had been tricked by the wise men, was in a furious rage, and he sent and killed all the male children in Bethlehem and in all that region who were two years old or under, according to the time which he had ascertained from the wise men.

Jn 3:20 — For every one who does evil hates the light, and does not come to the light, lest his deeds should be exposed.

Mk 3:6 — The Pharisees went out, and immediately held counsel with the Herodians against him, how to destroy him.

Mt. 12:34 — 'You brood of vipers! how can you speak good, when you are evil? For out of the abundance of the heart the mouth speaks.'

Mt. 13:38 — '. . . the field is the world, and the good seed means the sons of the kingdom; the weeds are the sons of the evil one . . . .'

Jn 6:70-71 — Jesus answered them, 'Did I not choose you, the twelve, and one of you is a devil?' He spoke of Judas the son of Simon Iscariot, for he, one of the twelve, was to betray him.

Mt. 16:23 — But he turned and said to Peter, 'Get behind me Satan. You are a hindrance to me; for you are not on the side of God, but of men.'

Jn 7:7 — 'The world cannot hate you, but it hates me because I testify of it that its works are evil.'

Jn 8:34 — Jesus answered them, 'Truly, truly, I say to you, every one who commits sin is a slave to sin.'

Jn 8:44 'You are of your father the devil, and your will is to do your father's desires.'

Jn 10:8 'All who came before me are thieves and robbers; but the sheep did not heed them.'

Jn 10:10 'The thief comes only to steal and kill and destroy; I came that they may have life, and have it abundantly.'

Lk. 13:31,32 At that very hour some Pharisees came, and said to him, 'Get away from here, for Herod wants to kill you.' And he said to them, 'Go and tell that fox, "Behold, I cast out demons and perform cures today and tomorrow, and the third day I finish my course." '

Mt. 23:15 'Woe to you, Scribes and Pharisees, hypocrites! for you traverse sea and land to make a single proselyte, and when he becomes a proselyte, you make him twice as much a child of hell as yourselves.'

Mt. 26:66-68 'What is your judgment?' They answered, 'He deserves death.' Then they spat in his face and struck him; and some slapped him, saying, 'Prophesy to us, you Christ! Who is it that struck you?'

Mt. 27:23 And he said, 'Why, what evil has he done?' But they shouted all the more, 'Let him be crucified.'

Mt. 27:43 He trusts in God; let God deliver him now, if he desires him; for he said, 'I am the Son of God.'

See also: 3. Our Saviour.

3. Our Saviour

i. Change of heart

<table>
<tr><td>Lk.
1:16,17</td><td>'And he will turn many of the sons of Israel to the Lord their God,
And he will go before him in the spirit and power of Elijah . . . .'</td></tr>
<tr><td>Lk.
3:3</td><td>. . . and he went into all the region about the Jordan, preaching a baptism of repentance for the forgiveness of sins.</td></tr>
<tr><td>Lk.
3:8-14</td><td>'Bear fruits that befit repentance, and do not begin to say to yourselves, "We have Abraham as our father;" for I tell you, God is able from these stones to raise up children to Abraham. Even now the axe is laid to the root of the trees; every tree therefore that does not bear good fruit is cut down and thrown into the fire.'
And the multitudes asked him, 'What then shall we do?' And he answered them, 'He who has two coats, let him share with him who has none; and he who has food, let him do likewise.' Tax collectors came to be baptised, and said to him, 'Teacher, what shall we do?' And he said to them, 'Collect no more than is appointed to you.' Soldiers also asked him, 'And we, what shall we do?' And he said to them, 'Rob no one by violence or by false accusation, and be content with your wages.'</td></tr>
<tr><td>Mk
1:15</td><td>'The time is fulfilled, and the kingdom of God is at hand; repent, and believe in the gospel.'</td></tr>
<tr><td>Mt.
11:20</td><td>Then he began to upbraid the cities where most of his mighty works had been done, because they did not repent.</td></tr>
<tr><td>Mt.
12:41</td><td>'The men of Nineveh will arise at the judgment of this generation and condemn it; for they repented at the preaching of Jonah, and behold, something greater than Jonah is here.'</td></tr>
<tr><td>Lk.
13:3-5</td><td>'I tell you, No; but unless you repent you will likewise perish. Or those eighteen upon whom the tower in Siloam fell and killed them, do you think that they were worse offenders than all the others who dwelt in Jerusalem? I</td></tr>
</table>

tell you, No; but unless you repent you will all likewise perish.'

Lk. 24:46,47 ... and said to them, 'Thus it is written, that the Christ should suffer and on the third day rise from the dead, and that repentance and forgiveness of sins should be preached in his name to all nations, beginning from Jerusalem.'

ii. The importance of choice

Mt. 5:29,30 'If your right eye causes you to sin, pluck it out and throw it away; it is better that you lose one of your members than that your whole body be thrown into hell. And if your right hand causes you to sin, cut it off and throw it away; it is better that you lose one of your members than that your whole body go into hell.'

Mt. 12:33-37 'Either make the tree good, and its fruit good: or make the tree bad, and its fruit bad: for the tree is known by its fruit. You brood of vipers: how can you speak good, when you are evil? For out of the abundance of the heart the mouth speaks. The good man out of his good treasure brings forth good, and the evil man out of his evil treasure brings back evil. I tell you on the day of judgment men will render an account for every careless word they utter; for by your words you will be justified, and by your words you will be condemned.'

Mt. 18:8,9 'And if your hand or your foot causes you to sin, cut it off and throw it from you; it is better for you to enter life maimed or lame than with two hands or two feet to be thrown into the eternal fire. And if your eye causes you to sin, pluck it out and throw it from you; it is better for you to enter life with one eye than with two eyes to be thrown into the hell of fire.'

Lk. 9:60-62 But he said to them 'Leave the dead to bury their own dead; but as for you, go and proclaim the kingdom of God.' Another said, 'I will follow you, Lord; but let me first say farewell to those at my home.' Jesus said to him, 'No one who puts his hand to the plough and looks back is fit for the kingdom of God.'

Mt. 12:30	'He who is not with me is against me, and he who does not gather with me scatters.'
Mt. 6:19-21	'Do not lay up for yourselves treasures on earth, where moth and rust consume and where thieves break in and steal, but lay up for yourselves treasures in heaven, where neither moth nor rust consumes and where thieves do not break in and steal. For where your treasure is, there will your heart be also.'
Lk. 12:51-53	'Do you think that I have come to give peace on earth? No, I tell you, but rather division; for henceforth in one house there will be five divided, three against two and two against three; they will be divided father against son and son against father, mother against daughter and daughter against her mother, mother-in-law against her daughter-in-law, and daughter-in-law against her mother-in-law.'
Mt. 22:2,3	'The kingdom of heaven may be compared to a king who gave a marriage feast for his son, and sent his servants to call those who were invited to the marriage feast; but they would not come.'
Lk. 14:26,27	'If any man comes to me and does not hate his own father and mother and wife and brothers and sisters, yes, and even his own life, he cannot be my disciple.'
Lk. 16:13	'No servant can serve two masters; for either he will hate one and love the other, or he will be devoted to one and despise the other. You cannot serve God and mammon.'
Mt. 10:38	'. . . he who does not take up his cross and follow me is not worthy of me.'
Mk 16:16	'He who believes and is baptised will be saved; but he who does not believe will be condemned.'

iii. Threats to contemporaries or to specific groups

Lk. 3:7-9	He said therefore to the multitudes that came out to be baptized by him, 'You brood of vipers! Who warned you to flee from the wrath to come? Bear fruits that befit repentance, and do not begin to say to yourselves, "We have Abraham as our father"; for I tell you God is able from these stones to raise up children to Abraham. Even now the axe is laid to the root of the trees; every tree

therefore that does not bear good fruit is cut down and thrown into the fire.'

Mt. 15:7-9 'You hypocrites! Well did Isaiah prophesy of you, when he said:

"This people honours me with their lips,
but their heart is far from me;
in vain do they worship me,
teaching as doctrines the precepts of men."'

Mt. 11:20-24 Then he began to upbraid the cities where most of his mighty works had been done, because they did not repent. 'Woe to you, Chorazin! woe to you, Bethsaida! for if the mighty works done in you had been done in Tyre and Sidon, they would have repented long ago in sackcloth and ashes. But I tell you, it shall be more tolerable on the day of judgment for Tyre and Sidon than for you. And you, Capernaum, will you be exalted to heaven? You shall be brought down to Hades. For if the mighty works done in you had been done in Sodom, it would have remained until this day. But I tell you that it shall be more tolerable on the day of judgment for the land of Sodom than for you.'

Jn 8:21-24 Again he said to them, 'I go away, and you will seek me and die in your sin; where I am going, you cannot come.' Then said the Jews, 'Will he kill himself, since he says, "Where I am going, you cannot come"?' He said to them, 'You are from below, I am from above; you are of this world, I am not of this world. I told you that you would die in your sins, for you will die in your sins unless you believe that I am he.'

Jn 8:43,44 'Why do you not understand what I say? It is because you cannot bear to hear my word. You are of your father the devil, and your will is to do your father's desires. He was a murderer from the beginning, and he has nothing to do with truth, because there is no truth in him. When he lies, he speaks to his own nature, for he is a liar and the father of lies.'

Jn 8:55 'But you have not known him; I know him. If I said, I do not know him, I should be a liar like you; but I do know him and I keep his word.'

Mt. 24:40,41 'Then two men will be in a field; one is taken and the other left. Two women will be grinding at the mill; one is taken and one is left.'

Lk. 19:41-44 And when he drew near and saw the city he wept over it, saying, 'Would that even today you knew the things that make for peace! But now they are hid from your eyes. For the day shall come upon you, when your enemies will cast up a bank about you and surround you, and hem you in on every side, and dash you to the ground, you and your children within you, and they will not leave one stone upon another in you; because you did not know the time of your visitation.'

Mt. 21:13-44 He said to them, 'It is written, "My house shall be called a house of prayer"; but you make it into a den of robbers.'

And the blind and the lame came to him in the temple, and he healed them. But when the chief priests and the scribes saw the wonderful things that he did, and the children crying out in the temple, 'Hosanna to the Son of David', they were indignant; and they said to him, 'Do you hear what they are saying?' And Jesus said to them, 'Yes; have you never read:

"Out of the mouths of babes and sucklings
thou has brought perfect praise"?'

And leaving them, he went out of the city to Bethany and lodged there.

In the morning, as he was returning to the city, he was hungry. And seeing a fig tree by the wayside he went to it, and found nothing on it but leaves only. And he said to it, 'May no fruit ever come from you again.' And the fig tree withered at once. When the disciples saw it they marvelled, saying, 'How did the fig tree wither at once?' And Jesus answered them 'Truly, I say to you, if you have faith and never doubt, you will not only do what has been done to the fig tree, but even if you say to this mountain, "Be taken up and cast into the sea," it will be done. And whatever you ask in prayer, you will receive, if you have faith.'

And when he entered the temple, the chief priests and the elders of the people came up to him as he was teaching, and said, 'By what authority are you doing these things, and who gave you this authority?' Jesus answered them, 'I also will ask you a question; and if you tell me the answer, then I also will tell you by what authority I do these things. The baptism of John, whence was it? From heaven or from men?' And they argued with one another, 'If we say, "From heaven," he will say to us, "Why then did you not believe him?" But if we say "From men," we are afraid of the multitude; for all hold that John was a prophet.' So they answered Jesus, 'We do not know.' And he said to them, 'Neither will I tell you by what authority I do these things.'

'What do you think? A man had two sons; and he went to the first and said, "Son, go and work in the vineyard today." And he answered, "I will not"; but afterward he repented and went. And he went to the second and said the same; and he answered, "I go, sir," but did not go. Which of the two did the will of his father?' They said, 'The first.' Jesus said to them, 'Truly, I say to you, the tax collectors and the harlots go into the kingdom of God before you. For John came to you in the way of righteousness, and you did not believe him, but the tax collectors and the harlots believed him; and even when you saw it, you did not afterward repent and believe him.'

'Hear another parable. There was a householder who planted a vineyard, and set a hedge around it, and dug a wine press in it, and built a tower, and let it out to tenants, and went into another country. When the season of fruit drew near, he sent his servants to the tenants, to get his fruit; and the tenants took his servants and beat one, killed another, and stoned another. Again he sent other servants, more than the first; and they did the same to them. Afterward he sent his son to them, saying, "They will respect my son." But when the tenants saw the son, they said to themselves, "This is the heir; come, let us kill him and have his inheritance." and they took him and cast him out of the vineyard, and killed him. When the owner of the vineyard comes, what will he do to those tenants?' They said to him, 'He will put those wretches to a miserable death, and let out the vineyard to other tenants who will give him the fruits in their seasons.'

Jesus said to them, 'Have you never read in the scriptures:

"The very stone which the builders rejected
has become the head of the corner;
this was the Lord's doing, and it is marvellous in our eyes"?

Therefore I tell you, the kingdom of God will be taken away from you and given to a nation producing the fruits of it. And he who falls on this stone will be broken to pieces; but when it falls on any one, it will crush him.'

Mt. 23:13-30

'But woe to you, scribes and Pharisees, hypocrites! because you shut the kingdom of heaven against men; for you neither enter yourselves, nor allow those who would enter to go in. Woe to you, scribes and Pharisees, hypocrites! for you traverse sea and land to make a single proselyte, and when he becomes a proselyte, you make him twice as much a child of hell as yourselves.

'Woe to you, blind guides, who say, "If any one swears by the temple, it is nothing; but if anyone swears by the gold of the temple, he is bound by his oath." You blind fools! For which is greater, the gold, or the temple that has made the gold sacred? And you say, "If any one swears by the altar, it is nothing; but if any one swears by the gift that is on the altar, he is bound by his oath." You blind men! For which is greater, the gift or the altar that makes the gift sacred? So he who swears by the altar, swears by it and by everything on it; and he who swears by the temple, swears by it and by him who dwells in it; and he who swears by heaven, swears by the throne of God and by him who sits upon it.

'Woe to you, scribes and Pharisees, hypocrites! for you tithe mint and dill and cummin, and have neglected the weightier matters of the law, justice and mercy and faith; these you ought to have done, without neglecting the others. You blind guides, straining out a gnat and swallowing a camel!

'Woe to you, scribes and Pharisees, hypocrites! for

you cleanse the outside of the cup and the plate, but inside they are full of extortion and rapacity. You blind Pharisees! first cleanse the inside of the cup and of the plate, that the outside may also be clean.

'Woe to you, scribes and Pharisees, hypocrites! for you are like white-washed tombs, which outwardly appear beautiful, but within they are full of dead men's bones and all uncleanness. So you also outwardly appear righteous to men, but within you are full of hypocrisy and iniquity.

'Woe to you, scribes and Pharisees, hypocrites! for you build the tombs of the prophets and adorn the monuments of the righteous, saying, "If we had lived in the days of our fathers, we would not have taken part with them in shedding the blood of the prophets." Thus you witness against yourselves, that you are the sons of those who murdered the prophets. Fill up, then, the measure of your fathers. You serpents, you brood of vipers, how are you to escape being sentenced to hell? Therefore I send you prophets, wise men and scribes, some of whom you will kill and crucify, and some you will scourge in your synagogues and persecute from town to town, that upon you may come all the righteous blood shed on earth, from the blood of innocent Abel to the blood of Zechariah the son of Barachiah, whom you murdered between the sanctuary and the alter. Truly, I say to you, all this will come upon this generation.

'O Jerusalem, Jerusalem, killing the prophets and stoning those who are sent to you. How often would I have gathered your children together as a hen gathers her brood under her wings, and you would not! Behold your house is forsaken and desolate. For I tell you, you will not see me again, until you say, "Blessed is he who comes in the name of the Lord." '

Mt. 24:15-31

'So when you see the desolating sacrilege spoken of by the prophet Daniel, standing in the holy place (let the reader understand), then let those who are in Judea flee to the mountains; let him who is on the housetop not go down to take what is in his house; and let him who is in the field not turn back to take his mantle. And alas for those who are with child and for those who give suck in those days! Pray that your flight may not be in winter or on a sabbath. For then there will be great tribulation, such as has not been from the beginning of the world until now, no, and never will be. And if those days had not been shortened, no human being would be saved; but for the sake of the elect those days will be shortened. Then if anyone says to you, "Lo, here is the Christ!" or, "There he is!" do not believe it. For false Christs and false prophets will arise and show great signs and wonders, so as to lead astray, if possible, even the elect. Lo, I have told you beforehand. So, if they say to you, "Lo, he is in the wilderness," do not go out! If they say, "Lo, he is in the inner rooms," do not believe it. For as the lightning comes from the east and shines as far as the west, so will be the coming of the Son of man. Wherever the body is, there the eagles will be gathered together.

'Immediately after the tribulation of those days the sun will be darkened, and the moon will not give its light, and the stars will fall from heaven, and the powers of the heavens will be shaken; then will appear the sign of the Son of man in heaven, and then all the tribes of the earth will mourn, and they will see the Son of man coming on the clouds of heaven with power and great glory; and he will send out his angels with a loud trumpet call, and they will gather his elect from the four winds, from one end of the earth to the other.'

Jn 14:30 'I will no longer talk much with you, for the ruler of this world is coming. He has no power over me . . . .'

Jn 15:22-25 'If I had not come and spoken to them, they would not have sin; but now they have no excuse for their sin. He who hates me hates my father also. If I had not done among them the works which no one else did, they would not have sin; but now they have seen and hated both me and my father. It is to fulfil the word that is written in their law, "They hated me without a cause." '

Jn 17:12 'While I was with them, I kept them in thy name, which thou hast given me; I have guarded them, and none of them is lost but the son of perdition, that the scripture might be fulfilled.'

Lk. 23:28-31 But Jesus turning to them said, 'Daughters of Jerusalem, do not weep for me, but weep for yourselves and for your children. For behold the days are coming when they will say, "Blessed are the barren, and the wombs that never bore, and the breasts that never gave suck!" Then they will begin to say to the mountains, "Fall on us"; and to the hills, "Cover us." For if they do this when the wood is green, what will happen when it is dry?'

iv. Threats to all men

Mt. 5:20-22 'For I tell you, unless your righteousness exceeds that of the scribes and Pharisees, you will never enter the kingdom of heaven. You have heard it said to the men of old, "You shall not kill; and whoever kills shall be liable to judgment." But I say to you that everyone who is angry with his brother shall be liable to judgment; whoever insults his brother shall be liable to the council and whoever says, "You fool!" shall be liable to the hell of fire.'

Mt. 7:13,14 'Enter by the narrow gate; for the gate is wide and the way easy, that leads to destruction, and those who enter by it are many. For the gate is narrow and the way is hard, that leads to life, and those who find it are few.'

Lk. 6:49 'But he who hears and does not do them is like a man who built a house on the ground without a foundation; against which the stream broke, and immediately it fell, and the ruin of that house was great.'

Mt. 13:12 'For to him who has more will be given, and he will have abundance; but from him who has not, even what he has will be taken away.'

Mt. 13:18-23 'Hear then the parable of the sower. When anyone hears the word of the kingdom and does not understand it, the evil one comes and snatches away what is sown in his heart; this is what was sown along the path. As for what was sown on rocky ground, this is he who hears the word and immediately receives it with joy; yet he has no root in himself, but endures for a while, and when tribulation or persecution arises on account of the word, immediately he falls away. As for what was sown among the thorns, this is he who hears the word, but the cares of the world and the delight in riches choke the word, and it proves unfruitful. As for what was sown on the good soil, this is he who hears the word and understands it; he indeed bears fruit, and yields, in one case a hundredfold, in another sixty, and in another thirty.'

Mt. 10:14,15 'And if any one will not receive you or listen to your words, shake off the dust from your feet as you leave that house or town. Truly, I say to you, it shall be more tolerable on the day of judgment for the land of Sodom and Gomorrah than for that town.'

Mt. 15:13 He answered, 'Every plant which my heavenly Father has not planted will be rooted up.'

Mk 8:36-38 'For what does it profit a man, to gain the whole world and forfeit his life? For what can a man give in return for his life? For whoever is ashamed of me and of my words in this adulterous and sinful generation, of him will the Son of man also be ashamed, when he comes in the glory of his Father with the holy angels.'

Mt. 18:3 'Truly, I say to you, unless you turn and become like children, you will never enter the kingdom of heaven.'

Mt. 18:6,7 '... but whoever causes one of these little ones who believe in me to sin, it would be better for him to have a great millstone fastened round his neck and to be drowned in the depth of the sea.

'Woe to the world for temptations to sin! For it is necessary that temptations come, but woe to the man by whom the temptation comes!

Mt. 18:34,35 'And in his anger his lord delivered him to the jailers, till he should pay all his debt. So also my heavenly Father will do to every one of you, if you do not forgive your brother from your heart.'

Jn 9:39-41 Jesus said, 'For judgment I came into this world, that those who do not see may see, and that those who see may become blind.' Some of the Pharisees near him heard this, and they said to him, 'Are we also blind?'

Jesus said to them, 'If you were blind, you would have no guilt; but now that you say "We see" your guilt remains.'

Lk. 10:10-12 'But whenever you enter a town and they do not receive you, go into its streets and say, "Even the dust of your town that clings to our feet, we wipe off against you; nevertheless know this, that the kingdom of God has come near." I tell you, it shall be more tolerable on that day for Sodom than for that town.'

Lk. 10:16 'He who hears you hears me, and he who rejects you rejects me, and he who rejects me rejects him who sent me.'

Mk 11:26 'And whenever you stand praying, forgive, if you have anything against any one; so that your Father also who is in heaven may forgive you your trespasses.'

Mt. 12:31,32 'Therefore I tell you, every sin and blasphemy will be forgiven men, but blasphemy against the Spirit will not be forgiven. And whoever says a word against the Son of man will be forgiven; but whoever speaks against the Holy Spirit will not be forgiven, either in this age or in the age to come.'

Mt. 12:39 '... but he answered them, "An evil and adulterous generation seek for a sign; but no sign shall be given to it except the sign of the prophet Jonah." '

Mt. 6:23 '... but if your eye is not sound, your whole body will be full of darkness. If then the light in you is darkness, how great is the darkness!'

Lk. 12:4,5 'I tell you, my friends, do not fear those who kill the body, and after that have no more that they can do. But I will warn you whom to fear: fear him who, after he has killed, has power to cast into hell; yes, I tell you, fear him!'

Lk. 12:9 '... but he who denies me before men will be denied before the angels of God.'

Lk. 12:20 'But God said to him, "Fool! This night your soul is required of you; and the things you have prepared, whose will they be?" '

Mk 13:35-37 'Watch therefore – for you do not know when the master of the house will come, in the evening or at midnight, or at the cockcrow, or in the morning – lest he come suddenly and find you asleep. And what I say to you all: Watch.'

Mt. 24:39-44 '. . . and they did not know until the flood came and swept them all away, so will be the coming of the Son of man. Then two men will be in the field; one is taken and one is left. Two women will be grinding at the mill; one is taken and one is left. Watch therefore for you do not know on what day your Lord is coming. But know this that if the householder had known in what part of the night the thief was coming, he would have watched and would not have let his house be broken into. Therefore you also must be ready; for the Son of man is coming at an hour you do not expect.'

Mt. 24:48-51 'But if that wicked servant says to himself, "My master is delayed," and begins to beat his fellow servants, and eats and drinks with the drunken, the master of that servant will come on a day when he does not expect him and at an hour he does not know, and he will punish him, and put him with the hypocrites; there men will weep and gnash their teeth.'

Lk. 12:47,48 'And that servant who knew his master's will, but did not make ready or act according to his will, shall receive a severe beating. But he who did not know, and did what deserved a beating, shall receive a light beating. Every one to whom much is given, of him will much be required; and of him to whom men commit much they will demand the more.'

Lk. 12:58,59 'As you go with your accuser before the magistrate, make an effort to settle with him on the way, lest he drag you to the judge, and the judge hand you over to the officer, and the officer put you in prison. I tell you, you will never get out till you have paid the very last copper.'

Lk. 13:6-9 And he told this parable: 'A man had a fig tree planted in his vineyard; and he came seeking fruit on it and found none. And he said to the vinedresser, "Lo, these three years I have come seeking fruit on this fig tree, and I find none. Cut it down; why should it use up the ground?" And he answered him, "Let it alone, sir, this year also, till

I dig about it and put on manure. And if it bears fruit next year, well and good; but if not you can cut it down." '

Lk. 13:23-30 And some one said to him, 'Lord, will those who are saved be few?' And he said to them, 'Strive to enter by the narrow door; for many, I tell you, will seek to enter and will not be able. When once the householder has risen up and shut the door, you will begin to stand outside and to knock at the door, saying, "Lord, open to us." He will answer you, "I do not know where you come from." Then you will begin to say, "We ate and drank in your presence, and you taught in our streets." But he will say, "I tell you, I do not know where you come from; depart from me, all you workers of iniquity!" There you will weep and gnash your teeth, when you see Abraham and Isaac and Jacob and all the prophets in the kingdom of God and yourselves thrust out. And men will come from east and west, and from north and south, and sit at table in the kingdom of God. And behold, some are last who will be first, and some are first who will be last.'

Mt. 7:22,23 'On that day many will say to me, "Lord, Lord, did we not prophesy in your name, and cast out demons in your name, and do many mighty works in your name?" And then I will declare to them, "I never knew you; depart from me you evildoers." '

Lk. 14:24 'For I tell you, none of these men who were invited shall taste my banquet.'

Mt. 5:19 'Whoever then relaxes one of the least of these commandments and teaches men so, shall be called least in the kingdom of heaven; but he who does them and teaches them shall be called great in the kingdom of heaven.'

Lk. 16:26 'And besides all this, between us and you a great chasm has been fixed, in order that those who would pass from here to you may not be able, and none may cross from there to us.'

Mt. 24:11,12 'And many false prophets will arise and lead many astray. And because wickedness is multiplied, most men's love will grow cold.'

Lk. 18:8	'I tell you, he will vindicate them speedily. Nevertheless, when the Son of man comes, will he find faith on earth?'
Mt. 19:23,24	And Jesus said to his disciples, 'Truly, I say to you, it will be hard for a rich man to enter the kingdom of heaven. Again I tell you, it is easier for a camel to go through the eye of a needle than for a rich man to enter the kingdom of God.'
Lk. 19:22	'He said to him, "I will condemn you out of your own mouth, you wicked servant! You knew that I was a severe man, taking up what I did not lay down, and reaping what I did not sow?" '
Lk. 19:26,27	'I tell you, that to every one who has more will be given; but from him who has not, even what he has will be taken away. But as for these enemies of mine, who did not want me to reign over them, bring them here and slay them before me.'
Mt. 25:30	'And cast the worthless servant into the outer darkness; there men will weep and gnash their teeth.'
Lk. 21:34,35	'But take heed to yourselves lest your hearts be weighed down with dissipation and drunkenness and cares of this life, and that day come before you suddenly like a snare; for it will come upon all who dwell upon the face of the whole earth.'
Mt. 25:11,12	Afterwards the other maidens came also, saying, 'Lord, Lord, open to us.' But he replied, 'Truly, I say to you I do not know you.'
Mt. 26:52	Then Jesus said to him, 'Put your sword back into its place; for all who take the sword will perish by the sword.'
Mk 16:16	'He who believes and is baptized will be saved; but he who does not believe will be condemned.'
Jn 15:2	'Every branch of mine that bears no fruit, he takes away, and every branch that does bear fruit he prunes that it may bear more fruit.'
Jn 15:22	'If I had not come and spoken to them, they would not have sin; but now they have no excuse for their sin.'

v. Threats of hell

Mt. 5:22 — 'But I say to you that everyone who is angry with his brother shall be liable to judgment; whoever insults his brother shall be liable to the council, and whoever says, "You fool", shall be liable to the hell of fire.'

Mt. 5:29,30 — 'If your right eye causes you to sin, pluck it out and throw it away; it is better that you lose one of your members than that your whole body be thrown into hell. And if your right hand causes you to sin, cut it off and throw it away; it is better that you lose one of your members than that your whole body go into hell.'

Mt. 13:30 — 'Let both grow together until the harvest; and at harvest time I will tell the reapers, "Gather the weeds first and bind them in bundles to be burned, but gather the wheat into my barn."'

Mt. 13:40-42 — 'Just as the weeds are gathered and burned with fire, so will it be at the close of the age. The Son of man will send his angels, and they will gather out of his kingdom all causes of sin and all evildoers, and throw them into the furnace of fire; there men will weep and gnash their teeth.'

Mt. 13:47-50 — 'Again, the kingdom of heaven is like a net which was thrown into the sea and gathered fish of every kind; when it was full, men drew it ashore and sat down and sorted the good into vessels but threw away the bad. So will it be at the close of the age. The angels will come out and separate the evil from the righteous, and throw them into the furnace of fire; there men will weep and gnash their teeth.'

Mk 9:42-48 — 'Whoever causes one of these little ones who believe in me to sin, it would be better for him if a great millstone were hung round his neck and he were thrown into the sea. And if your hand causes you to sin, cut it off; it is better for you to enter life maimed than with two hands to go to hell, to the unquenchable fire. And if your foot causes you sin, cut it off; it is better for you to enter life lame, than with two feet to be thrown into hell. And if your eye causes you to sin, pluck it out; it is better for you to enter the kingdom of God with one eye than with two eyes to be thrown into hell, where the worm does not die, and the fire is not quenched.'

Lk. 14:34,35 'Salt is good; but if salt has lost its taste, how shall its saltness be restored? it is fit neither for the land nor for the dunghill; men throw it away. He who has ears to hear, let him hear.'

Mt. 11:23 'And you, Capernaum, will you be exalted to heaven? You shall be brought down to Hades. For if the mighty works done in you had been done in Sodom, it would have remained until this day.'

Lk. 12:5 'But I will warn you whom to fear: fear him who, after he has killed, has power to cast into hell; yes, I tell you, fear him!'

Mt. 23:15 'Woe to you, scribes and Pharisees, hypocrites! for you traverse sea and land to make a single proselyte, and when he becomes a proselyte you make him twice as much a child of hell as yourselves.'

Mt. 23:33 'You serpents, you brood of vipers, how are you to escape being sentenced to hell?'

Mt. 25:41 'Then he will say to those at his left hand, "Depart from me, you cursed, into the eternal fire prepared for the devil and his angels . . . ."'

Mt. 25:45 Then he answered them, 'Truly, I say to you, as you did it not to one of the least of these, you did it not to me.'

Jn 15:6 'If a man does not abide in me, he is cast forth as a branch and withers; and the branches are gathered, thrown into the fire and burned.'

vi. Judgement

Lk. 2:34,35 . . . and Simeon blessed them and said to Mary his mother,

'Behold, this child is set for the fall and rising of many
in Israel, and for a sign that is spoken against
(and a sword will pierce through your own soul also),
that thoughts out of many hearts may be revealed.'

Lk. 3:9 'Even now the axe is laid to the root of the trees; every tree therefore that does not bear good fruit is cut down and thrown into the fire.'

Lk. 3:17 'His winnowing fork is in his hand, to clear his threshing floor, and to gather the wheat into his granary, but the chaff he will burn with unquenchable fire.'

Mt. 5:20-22 For I tell you, unless your righteousness exceeds that of the scribes and Pharisees, you will never enter the kingdom of heaven. You have heard it was said to men of old, "You shall not kill; and whoever kills shall be liable to judgment." But I say to you, everyone who is angry with his brother shall be liable to judgment; whoever insults his brother shall be liable to the council, and whoever says, "You fool!" shall be liable to the fires of hell.'

Mt. 12:37 '. . . for by your words you will be justified, and by your words you will be condemned.'

Mt. 13:13-15 'This is why I speak to them in parables, because seeing they do not see, and hearing they do not hear, nor do they understand. With them indeed is fulfilled the prophecy of Isaiah which says:

"You shall hear indeed but never understand,
and you shall indeed see but never perceive.
For this people's heart has grown dull,
and their ears are heavy of hearing,
and their eyes they have closed,
lest they should perceive with their eyes,
and hear with their ears,
and understand with their hearts,
and turn for me to heal them."'

Jn 5:22 'The Father judges no one, but has given all judgment to the Son.'

Jn 5:24 'Truly, truly, I say to you, he who hears my word and believes him who sent me, has eternal life; he does not come into judgment, but has passed from death to life.'

Jn 5:26-29 'For as the Father has life in himself, so he has granted the Son also to have life in himself, and he has given him authority to execute judgment, because he is the Son of man. Do not marvel at this; for the hour is coming when all who are in the tombs will hear his voice and come forth, those who have done good, to the resurrection of life, and those who have done evil, to the resurrection of judgment.'

Jn 5:45	'Do not think that I shall accuse you to the Father; it is Moses who accuses you, on whom you set your hope.'
Mt. 11:24	'But I tell you that it shall be more tolerable on the day of judgment for the land of Sodom than for you.'
Jn 8:15,16	'You judge according to the flesh, I judge no one. Yet even if I do judge, my judgment is true, for it is not I alone who judge, but I and he who sent me.'
Jn 8:50	'Yet I do not seek my own glory; there is One who seeks it and he will be the judge.'
Jn 9:39	Jesus said, 'For judgment I came into this world, that those who do not see may see, and that those who see may become blind.'
Jn 12:31	'Now is the judgment of this world, now shall the ruler of this world be cast out; and I, when I am lifting up from the earth, will draw all men to myself.'
Jn 12:47,48	'If anyone hears my sayings and does not keep them, I do not judge him; for I did not come to judge the world but to save the world. He who rejects me and does not receive my sayings has a judge; the word that I have spoken will be his judge on the last day.'
Lk. 21:36	'But watch at all times, praying that you may have strength to escape all these things that will take place, and to stand before the Son of Man.'
Mt. 25:31	'When the Son of man comes in his glory, and all the angels with him, then will he sit on his glorious throne . . . .'
Jn 16:11	'. . . of judgment, because the ruler of this world is judged.'
Mt. 26:64	Jesus said to him, 'You have said so. But I tell you, hereafter you will see the Son of man seated at the right hand of Power, and coming on the clouds of heaven.'

vii. Salvation, Forgiveness, Mercy, Redemption

Lk. 1:50-55 'And his mercy is on those who fear him
from generation to generation.
He has shown strength with his arm,

he has scattered the proud in the imagination of their hearts,
he has put down the mighty from their thrones,
and exalted those of low degree;
he has filled the hungry with good things,
and the rich has sent empty away.
He has helped his servant Israel,
in remembrance of his mercy,
as he spoke to our fathers,
to Abraham and to his posterity for ever.'

Lk. 1:68-79 'Blessed be the God of Israel,
for he has visited and redeemed his people,
and he has raised up a horn of salvation for us
in the house of his servant David,
as he spoke by the mouth of his holy prophets from of old,
that we should be saved from our enemies,
and from the hand of all who hate us;
to perform the mercy promised to our fathers,
and to remember his holy covenant,
the oath which he swore to our father Abraham, to grant us
that we, being delivered from the hand of our enemies,
might serve him without fear,
in holiness and righteousness before him all the days of our life.
And you, child, will be called the prophet of the Most High;
for you will go before the Lord to prepare his ways,
to give knowledge of salvation to his people
in the forgiveness of their sins,
through the tender mercy of our God,
when the day shall down upon us from on high
to give light to those who sit in darkness and in the shadow of death
to guide our feet into the way of peace.'

Mt. 1:21 '... she will bear a son, and you shall call his name Jesus,
for he will save his people from their sins.'

Lk. 2:11 '... for to you is born this day in the city of David a Saviour, who is Christ the Lord.'

Lk. 2:29-32

'Lord, now lettest thou thy servant depart in peace, according to thy word;
for mine eyes have seen thy salvation which thou hast prepared in the presence of all peoples,
a light for revelation to the Gentiles, and for glory to thy people Israel.'

Lk. 3:6

'. . . and all flesh shall see the salvation of God.'

Jn 4:22

'You worship what you do not know; we worship what we know, for salvation is from the Jews.'

Jn 4:42

They said to the woman, 'It is no longer because of your words that we believe, for we have heard for ourselves, and we know that this is indeed the Saviour of the world.'

Lk. 4:17-21

. . . and there was given to him the book of the prophet Isaiah. He opened the book and found the place where it was written,

'the Spirit of the Lord is upon me,
because he has anointed me to preach the good news to the poor.
He has sent me to proclaim release to the captives
and recovering of sight to the blind,
to set at liberty those who are oppressed,
to proclaim the acceptable year of the Lord.'

And he closed the book and gave it back to the attendant, and sat down; and the eyes of all who were in the synagogue were fixed on him. And he began to say to them, 'Today this scripture has been fulfilled in your hearing.'

Lk. 5:20-24

And when he saw their faith he said, 'Man, your sins are forgiven you.' And the scribes and the Pharisees began to question, saying, 'Who is this who speaks blasphemies? Who can forgive sins but God only?' When Jesus perceived their questionings, he answered them, 'Why do you question in your hearts? Which is easier, to say, "Your sins are forgiven you," or to say "Rise and walk"? But that you may know that the Son of man has authority on earth to forgive sins' – he said to the man who was paralysed – 'I say to you, rise, take up your bed and go home.'

Mt. 9:12,13 But when he heard it, he said, 'Those who are well have no need of a physician, but those who are sick. Go and learn what this means, "I desire mercy, and not sacrifice." For I came not to call the righteous but sinners.'

Mt. 4:21 And going on from there he saw two other brothers, James the son of Zebedee and John his brother, in the boat with Zebedee their father, mending their nets, and he called them.

Lk. 7:47-49 'Therefore I tell you, her sins, which are many, are forgiven, for she loved much; but he who is forgiven little, loves little.' And he said to her, 'Your sins are forgiven.' Then those who were at table with him began to say among themselves, 'Who is this, who even forgives sins?'

Jn 6:37-39 'All that the Father gives me will come to me; and he who comes to me I will not cast out. For I have come down from heaven, not to do my own will, but the will of him who sent me; and this is the will of him who sent me, that I should lose nothing of all that he has given, but raise it up at the last day.'

Jn 5:34 'Not that the testimony which I receive is from man; but I say this that you may be saved.'

Mt. 16:18,19 'And I tell you, you are Peter, and on this rock I will build my church, and the powers of death shall not prevail against it. It will give you the keys of the kingdom of heaven, and whatever you bind on earth shall be bound in heaven, and whatever you loose on earth shall be loosed in heaven.'

Mt. 18:11-14 'What do you think? If a man has a hundred sheep, and one of them has gone astray, does he not leave the other ninety-nine on the hills and go in search of the one that went astray? And if he finds it, I say to you, he will rejoice over it more than over the ninety-nine that never went astray. So it is not the will of my Father who is in heaven that one of these little ones should perish.'

Jn 8:7-11 And as they continued to ask him, he stood up and said to them, 'Let him who is without sin among you be the first to throw a stone at her.' And once more he bent down and wrote with his finger on the ground. But when they heard it, they went away, one by one, beginning with the eldest, and Jesus was left alone with the woman standing before him. Jesus looked up and said to her, 'Woman, where are they? Has no one condemened you?' She said, 'No one, Lord' And Jesus said, 'Neither do I condemn you; go and do not sin again.'

Mt. 12:31,32 'Therefore I tell you, every sin and blasphemy will be forgiven men, but blasphemy against the Spirit will not be forgiven. And whoever says a word against the Son of man will be forgiven; but whoever speaks against the Holy Spirit will not be forgiven, either in this age or in the age to come.'

Jn 10:27,28 'My sheep hear my voice, and I know them, and they follow me; and I give them eternal life, and they shall never perish, and no one shall snatch them out of my hand.'

Lk. 13:34 'O Jerusalem, Jerusalem, killing the prophets and stoning those who are sent to you! How often would I have gathered your children together as a hen gathers her brood under her wings, and you would not!'

Lk. 14:5 And he said to them, 'Which of you, having an ass or an ox that has fallen into a well, will not immediately pull him out on a sabbath day?'

Lk. 15:3-10 So he told them this parable: 'What man of you, having a hundred sheep, if he had lost one of them, does not leave the ninety-nine in the wilderness, and go after the one which is lost, until he finds it? And when he has found it, he lays it on his shoulders, rejoicing. And when he comes home, he calls together his friends and his neighbours, saying to them, "Rejoice with me, for I have found my sheep which was lost." Just so, I tell you, there will be more joy in heaven over one sinner who repents than over ninety-nine righteous persons who have no need of repentance.

'Or what woman, having ten silver coins, if she loses one coin, does not light a lamp and sweep the house and seek diligently until she finds it? And when she has found it, she calls together her friends and neighbours, saying,

"Rejoice with me, for I have found the coin which I had lost." Just so, I tell you, there is joy before the angels of God over one sinner who repents.'

Lk. 15:11-32

And he said, 'There was a man who had two sons; and the younger of them said to his father, "Father, give me the share of property that falls to me." And he divided his living between them. Not many days later, the younger son gathered all he had and took his journey into a far country, and there he squandered his property in loose living. And when he had spent everything, a great famine arose in that country, and he began to be in want. So he went and joined himself to one of the citizens of that country, who sent him into his fields to feed swine. And he would have gladly have fed on pods that the swine ate; and no one gave him anything. But when he came to himself he said, "How many of my father's hired servants have bread enough to spare, but I perish here with hunger! I will arise and go to my father, and I will say to him, 'Father, I have sinned against heaven and before you; I am no longer worthy to be called your son; treat me as one of your hired servants.'" And he arose and came to his father. But while he was yet at a distance, his father saw him and had compassion, and he ran and embraced him and kissed him. And the son said to him, "Father, I have sinned against heaven and before you; I am no longer worthy to be called your son." But the father said to his servants, "Bring quickly the best robe, and put it on him; and put a ring on his hand, and shoes on his feet; and bring the fatted calf and kill it, and let us eat and make merry; for this my son was dead, and is alive again; he was lost, and is found." And they began to make merry.

'Now his elder son was in the field; and as he came and drew near to the house, he heard music and dancing. And he called one of the servants and asked what this meant. And he said to him, "Your brother has come, and your father has killed the fatted calf, because he has received him safe and sound." But he was angry and refused to go in. His father came out and entreated him, but he answered his father, "Lo, these many years I have served you, and I never disobeyed your command; yet you never gave me a kid that I might make merry with my friends. But when this son of yours came, who has devoured your living with harlots, you killed for him the fatted calf." And he said to him, "Son, you are always with me, and all that is mine is yours. It was fitting to make merry and be glad, for this your brother was dead, and is alive; he was lost, and is found."'

Mk 10:26,27	'Then who can be saved?' Jesus looked at them and said, 'With men it is impossible, but not with God.'
Mk 10:45	'For the Son of man also came not to be served but to serve, and to give his life as a ransom for many.'
Lk. 19:9,10	And Jesus said to him, 'Today salvation has come to this house, since he also is a son of Abraham. For the Son of man came to seek and save the lost.'
Jn 12:31,32	'Now is the judgment of this world, now shall the ruler of this world be cast out, and I when I am lifted up from the earth, will draw all men to myself.'
Mt. 24:13	'But he who endures to the end will be saved.'
Mt. 26:28	'. . . for this is my blood of the covenant, which is poured out for many for the forgiveness of sins.'
Lk. 22:61,62	And Jesus said, 'Father, forgive them; for they know not what they do.'
Lk. 23:43	And he said to him, 'Truly, I say to you, today you will be with me in Paradise.'
Lk. 24:21	'But we had hoped that he was the one to redeem Israel. Yes, and besides all this, it is now the third day since this happened.'
Lk. 24:46,47	. . . and said to them, 'Thus it is written, that the Christ should suffer and on the third day rise from the dead, and that repentance and forgiveness of sins should be preached in his name to all nations beginning from Jerusalem.'

See also: 2. Our Enemy
10.i. Lack of Faith is blameworthy
18. Failures that provoke Christ.

4. Jesus: He is from God

i. Jesus is sent from God

Lk. 1:43 — 'And why is this granted me, that the mother of my Lord should come to me?'

Lk. 2:11 — '. . . for to you is born this day in the city of David a Saviour, who is Christ the Lord.'

Lk. 2:26 — And it had been revealed to him by the Holy Spirit that he should not see death before he had seen the Lord's Christ.

Lk. 2:32 — '. . . a light for revelation to the Gentiles, and for glory to thy people Israel.'

Mt. 3:3 — For this is he who was spoken of by the prophet Isaiah when he said, 'The voice of one crying in the wilderness: prepare the way of the Lord, make his paths straight.'

Jn 1:23 — He said, 'I am the voice of one crying in the wilderness, "Make straight the way of the Lord", as the prophet Isaiah said.'

Jn 1:29 — The next day he saw Jesus coming toward him, and said, 'Behold, the Lamb of God, who takes away the sin of the world!'

Jn 1:33 — 'I myself did not know him; but he who sent me to baptize with water said to me, "He on whom you see the spirit descend and remain, this is he who baptizes with the Holy Spirit." '

Jn 1:36 — . . . and he looked at Jesus as he walked, and said, 'Behold, the lamb of God!'

Jn 1:41 — He first found his brother Simon, and said to him, 'We have found the Messiah' (which means Christ).

Jn 1:45 — Philip found Nathanael, and said to him, 'We have found him of whom Moses in the law and also the prophets wrote, Jesus of Nazareth, the son of Joseph.'

Jn 3:28-29 — '. . . You yourselves bear me witness, that I said, I am not the Christ, but I have been sent before him. He who has the bride is the bridegroom; the friend of the bridegroom, who stands and hears him, rejoices greatly at the bridegroom's voice; therefore this joy of mine is now full.'

Jn 4,25,26	The woman said to him, 'I know that Messiah is coming (he who is called Christ); when he comes, he will show us all things.' Jesus said to her, 'I who speak to you am he.'
Mk 1:23,24	And immediately there was in their synagogue a man with an unclean spirit; and he cried out, 'What have you to do with us, Jesus of Nazareth? Have you come to destroy us? I know who you are, the Holy One of God.'
Lk. 4:41	And demons also came out of many, crying, 'You are the Son of God.' But he rebuked them, and would not allow them to speak, because they knew that he was the Christ.
Jn 6:44	'. . . No one can come to me unless the Father who sent me draws him; and I will raise him up at the last day.'
Jn 6:46	'. . . Not that anyone has seen the Father except him who is from God; he has seen the Father.'
Jn 6:57	'As the living Father sent me, and I live because of the Father, so he who eats me will live because of me.'
Jn 6:58	'This is the bread which came down from heaven, not such as the fathers ate and died; he who eats this bread will live for ever.'
Jn 6:69	'. . . and we have believed, and have come to know, that you are the Holy One of God.'
Jn 5:32	'. . . there is another who bears witness to me, and I know that the testimony which he bears to me is true.'
Jn 5:36-38	'. . . But the testimony which I have is greater than that of John; for the works which the Father has granted me to accomplish, these very works which I am doing, bear me witness that the Father has sent me. And the Father who sent me has himself borne witness to me. His voice you have heard, his form you have never seen; and you do not have his word abiding in you, for you do not believe him whom he has sent.'
Jn 5:43	'. . . I have come in my Father's name, and you do not receive me; if another comes in his own name, him you will receive.'
Mt. 16:20	Then he strictly charged the disciples to tell no one that he was the Christ.

Jn 7:18	'... He who speaks on his own authority seeks his own glory; but he who seeks the glory of him who sent him is true, and in him there is no falsehood.'
Jn 7:28,29	So Jesus proclaimed, as he taught in the temple, 'You know me, and you know where I come from? But I have not come of my own accord; he who sent me is true, and him you do not know. I know him, for I come from him, and he sent me.'
Jn 8:16-18	'... Yet even if I do judge, my judgment is true, for it is not I alone that judge, but I and he who sent me. In your law it is written that the testimony of two men is true; I bear witness to myself, and the Father who sent me bears witness to me.'
Jn 8:23	He said to them, 'You are from below, I am from above; you are of this world, I am not of this world.'
Jn 8:26,27	'... I have much to say about you and much to judge; but he who sent me is true, and I declare to the world what I have heard from him.' They did not understand that he spoke to them of the Father.
Jn 8:42	Jesus said to them, 'If God were your Father, you would love me, for I proceeded and came forth from God; I came not of my own accord, but he sent me.'
Lk. 10:16	'He who hears you hears me, and he who rejects you rejects me, and he who rejects me rejects him who sent me.'
Jn 11:27	She said to him, 'Yes, Lord; I believe that you are the Christ, the Son of God, he who is coming into the world.'
Jn 11:50-52	'... you do not understand that it is expedient for you that one man should die for the people, and that the whole nation should not perish.' He did not say this of his own accord, but being high priest that year he prophesied that Jesus should die for the nation, and not for the nation only, but to gather into one the children of God who are scattered abroad.
Mk 11:9,10	And those who went before and those who followed cried out, 'Hosanna! Blessed is he who comes in the name of the Lord! Blessed is the kingdom of our Father David that is coming! Hosanna in the highest!'

Lk. 20:41-44	But he said to them, 'How can they say that the Christ is David's son? For David himself says in the Book of Psalms, "The Lord said to my Lord, Sit at my right hand, till I make thy enemies a stool for thy feet." David thus calls him Lord; so how is he his son?'
Mt. 23:10	'. . . Neither be called masters, for you have one master, the Christ.'
Mk 13:32	'But of that day or that hour no one knows, not even the angels in heaven, nor the Son, but only the Father.'
Jn 13:13	'. . . You call me Teacher and Lord; and you are right, for so I am.'
Jn 14:24	'. . . He who does not love me does not keep my words; and the word which you hear is not mine but the Father's who sent me.'
Jn 15:23,24	'. . . He who hates me hates my Father also. If I had not done among them the works which no one else did, they would not have sin; but now they have seen and hated both me and my Father.'
Mt. 26:53	'. . . Do you think that I cannot appeal to my Father, and he will at once send me more than twelve legions of angels?'
Lk. 23:35-37	And the people stood by, watching; but the rulers scoffed at him, saying, 'He saved others; let him save himself, if he is the Christ of God, his Chosen One!' The soldiers also mocked him, coming up and offering him vinegar, and saying, 'If you are the King of the Jews, save yourself!'
Mt. 27:43	'. . . He trusts in God; let God deliver him now, if he desires him; for he said, "I am the Son of God."'
Mk 16:19	So then the Lord Jesus, after he had spoken to them, was taken up into heaven, and sat down at the right hand of God.

ii. Jesus is Son of God

Lk. 1:32	'. . . He will be great, and will be called the Son of the Most High; and the Lord God will give to him the throne of his father David . . . .'

Lk. 1:35	And the angel said to her, 'The Holy Spirit will come upon you, and the power of the Most High will overshadow you; therefore the child to be born will be called holy, the Son of God.'
Mt. 1:20	But as he considered this, behold an angel of the Lord appeared to him in a dream, saying, 'Joseph, son of David, do not fear to take Mary your wife, for that which is conceived in her is of the Holy Spirit . . . .'
Mt. 2:15	This was to fulfil what the Lord had spoken by the prophet, 'Out of Egypt have I called my son.'
Lk. 2:49	And he said to them, 'How is it that you sought me? Did you not know that I must be in my Father's House?'
Mt. 3:17	'This is my beloved Son, with whom I am well pleased.'
Lk. 4:3	The devil said to him, 'If you are the Son of God, command this stone to become bread.'
Lk. 4:9	And he took him to Jerusalem, and set him on the pinnacle of the temple, and said to him, 'If you are the Son of God, throw yourself down from here . . . .'
Jn 1:34	'. . . And I have seen and have borne witness that this is the Son of God.'
Jn 1:49	Nathanael answered him, 'Rabbi, you are the Son of God! You are the King of Israel!'
Jn 2:16	And he told those who sold the pigeons, 'Take these things away; you shall not make my Father's house a house of trade.'
Jn 3:16-18	For God so loved the world that he gave his only Son, that whoever believes in him should not perish but have eternal life. For God sent the Son into the world, not to condemn the world, but that the world might be saved through him. He who believes in him is not condemned; he who does not believe is condemned already, because he has not believed in the name of the only Son of God.
Mk 3:11,12	And whenever the unclean spirits beheld him, they fell down before him and cried out, 'You are the Son of God'. And he strictly ordered them not to make him known.

Mt. 8:29 — And behold they cried out, 'What have you to do with us, O Son of God? Have you come here to torment us before the time?'

Mt. 14:33 — And those in the boat worshipped him, saying, 'Truly you are the Son of God.'

Mt. 16:16 — Simon Peter replied, 'You are the Christ, the Son of the living God.'

Jn 6:57,58 — 'As the living Father sent me, and I live because of the Father, so he who eats me will live because of me. This is the bread which came down from heaven, not such as the fathers ate and died; he who eats this bread will live for ever.'

Jn 5:17-30 — But Jesus answered them, 'My Father is working still, and I am working.' This is why the Jews sought all the more to kill him, because he not only broke the sabbath but also called God his Father, making himself equal with God.

Jesus said to them, 'Truly, truly, I say to you, the Son can do nothing of his own accord, but only what he sees the Father doing: for whatever he does, that the Son does likewise. For the Father loves the Son, and shows him all that he himself is doing; and greater works than these will he show him, that you may marvel. For as the Father raises the dead and gives them life, so also the Son gives life to whom he will. The Father judges no one, but has given all judgment to the Son, that all may honour the Son, even as they honour the Father. He who does not honour the Son does not honour the Father who sent him. Truly, truly, I say to you, he who hears my word and believes him who sent me, has eternal life; he does not come into judgment, but has passed from death to life.

'Truly, truly, I say to you, the hour is coming, and now is, when the dead will hear the voice of the Son of God, and those who hear will live. For as the Father has life in himself, so he has granted the Son also to have life in himself, and has given him authority to execute judgment, because he is the Son of man. Do not marvel at this; for the hour is coming when all who are in the tombs will hear his voice and come forth, those who have done good, to the resurrection of life, and those who have done evil, to the resurrection of judgment.'

Mt. 16:16 Simon Peter replied, 'You are the Christ, the Son of the living God.'

Mt. 17:5 He was still speaking, when lo, a bright cloud overshadowed them, and a voice from the cloud said, 'This is my beloved Son, with whom I am well pleased; listen to him.'

Jn 8:16-19 '. . . Yet even if I do judge, my judgment is true, for it is not I alone that judge, but I and he who sent me. In your law it is written that the testimony of two men is true; I bear witness to myself, and the Father who sent me bears witness to me.' They said to him therefore, 'Where is your Father?' Jesus answered, 'You know neither me nor my Father; if you knew me, you would know my Father also.'

Jn 8:26-28 '. . . I have much to say about you and much to judge; but he who sent me is true, and I declare to the world what I have heard from him.' They did not understand that he spoke to them of the Father. So Jesus said, 'When you have lifted up the Son of man, then you will know that I am he, and that I do nothing on my own authority but speak thus as the Father taught me.'

Jn 8:49 Jesus answered, 'I have not a demon; but I honour my Father, and you dishonour me.'

Jn 9:35 Jesus heard that they had cast him out, and having found him he said, 'Do you believe in the Son of man?'

Jn 11:27 She said to him, 'Yes, Lord; I believe that you are the Christ, the Son of God, he who is coming into the world.'

Jn 13:1 Now before the feast of the Passover, when Jesus knew that his hour had come to depart out of this world to the Father, having loved his own who were in the world, he loved them to the end.

Jn 19:7 The Jews answered him, 'We have a law, and by that law he ought to die, because he has made himself the Son of God.'

Lk. 23:26	And as they led him away, they seized one Simon of Cyrene, who was coming in from the country, and laid on him the cross, to carry it behind Jesus.
Mt. 27:43	'. . . He trusts in God; let God deliver him now, if he desires him; for he said, "I am the Son of God".'
Mt. 27:54	When the centurion and those who were with him, keeping watch over Jesus, saw the earthquake and what took place, they were filled with awe, and said, 'Truly, this was the Son of God!'
Jn 20:17	Jesus said to her, 'Do not hold me, for I have not yet ascended to the Father; but go to my brethren and say to them, I am ascending to my Father and your Father, to my God and your God.'

iii. Jesus is God

Jn 1:1,2	In the beginning was the Word, and the Word was with God, and the Word was God. He was in the beginning with God . . . .'
Lk. 5:21-24	And the scribes and the Pharisees began to question, saying, 'Who is this that speaks of blasphemies? Who can forgive sins but God only?' When Jesus perceived their questionings, he answered them 'Why do you question in your hearts? Which is easier to say, "Your sins are forgiven you", or to say, "Rise and walk"? But that you may know that the Son of man has authority on earth to forgive sins' – he said to the man who was paralysed – 'I say to you, rise, take up your bed and go home.'
Jn 5:17-30	But Jesus answered them, 'My Father is working still, and I am working.' This is why the Jews sought all the more to kill him, because he not only broke the sabbath but also called God his Father, making himself equal with God. Jesus said to them, 'Truly, truly, I say to you, the Son can do nothing of his own accord, but only what he sees the Father doing: for whatever he does, that the Son does likewise. For the Father loves the Son, and shows him all that he himself is doing; and greater works than these will he show him, that you may marvel. For as the

Father raises the dead and gives them life, so also the Son gives life to whom he will. The Father judges no one, but has given all judgment to the Son, that all may honour the Son, even as they honour the Father. He who does not honour the Son does not honour the Father who sent him. Truly, truly, I say to you, he who hears my word and believes him who sent me, has eternal life; he does not come into judgment, but has passed from death to life.

'Truly, truly, I say to you, the hour is coming, and now is, when the dead will hear the voice of the Son of God, and those who hear will live. For as the Father has life in himself, so he has granted the Son also to have life in himself, and has given him authority to execute judgment, because he is the Son of man. Do not marvel at this; for the hour is coming when all who are in the tombs will hear his voice and come forth, those who have done good, to the resurrection of life, and those who have done evil, to the resurrection of judgment.'

Jn 5:22,23 '. . . The Father judges no one, but has given all judgment to the Son, that all may honour the Son, even as they honour the Father. He who does not honour the Son does not honour the Father who sent him.'

Jn 5:26 '. . . For as the Father has life in himself, so he has granted the Son also to have life in himself . . . .'

Jn 8:52 '. . . and you say, "If any one keeps my word, he will never taste death."'

Jn 8:56-58 '. . . Your Father Abraham rejoiced that he was to see my day; he saw it and was glad.' The Jews then said to him, 'You are not yet fifty years old, and have you seen Abraham?' Jesus said to them, 'Truly, truly, I say to you, before Abraham was, I am.'

Mt. 11:27 'All things have been delivered to me by my Father; and no one knows the Son except the Father; and no one knows the Father except the Son and any one to whom the Son chooses to reveal him.'

Jn 10:30 '. . . I and the Father are one.'

Jn 10:36-38 '. . . do you say of him whom the Father consecrated and sent into the world, "You are blaspheming," because I said "I am the Son of God"? If I am not doing the works of my Father, then do not believe me; but if I do them, even though you do not believe me, believe the works, that you may know and understand that the Father is in me and I am in the Father.'

Jn 14:6-14 Jesus said to him, 'I am the way, and the truth, and the life; no one comes to the Father, but by me. If you had known me, you would have known my Father also; henceforth you know him and have seen him.'

Philip said to him, 'Lord, show us the Father, and we shall be satisfied.' Jesus said to him, 'Have I been with you so long, and yet you do not know me Philip? He who has seen me has seen the Father; how can you say, "Show us the Father"? Do you not believe that I am in the Father and the Father in me? The words that I say to you I do not speak on my own authority; but the Father who dwells in me does his works. Believe me that I am in the Father and the Father in me; or else believe me for the sake of the works themselves.

'Truly, truly, I say to you, he who believes in me will also do the works that I do; and greater works than these will he do, because I go to the Father. Whatever you ask in my name, I will do it, that the Father may be glorified in the Son; if you ask anything in my name, I will do it.'

Jn 16:15 '. . . All that the Father has is mine; therefore I said that he will take what is mine and declare it to you.'

Jn 17:3 '. . . And this is eternal life, that they know thee the only true God, and Jesus Christ whom thou hast sent.'

Jn 20:28 Thomas answered him, 'My Lord and my God'.

Mt. 28:18,19 And Jesus came and said unto them, 'All authority in heaven and on earth has been given to me. Go therefore and make disciples of all nations, baptizing them in the name of the Father and of the Son and of the Holy Spirit . . . .'

iv. Jesus reveals the Father: Glory

Jn 1:14 — And the Word became flesh and dwelt among us, full of grace and truth; we have beheld its glory, glory as of the only Son from the Father.

Jn 1:18 — No one has ever seen God; the only Son, who is in the bosom of the Father, he has made him known.

Mt. 1:23 — 'Behold, a virgin shall conceive and bear a son,
and his name shall be called Emmanuel'
(which means, God with us).

Jn 3:31-34 — He who comes from above is above all; he who is of the earth belongs to the earth, and of the earth he speaks; he who comes from heaven is above all. He bears witness to what he has seen and heard, yet no one receives his testimony; he who receives his testimony sets his seal to this, that God is true. For he whom God has sent utters the words of God, for it is not by measure that he gives the Spirit . . . .

Mt. 12:18 — 'Behold my servant whom I have chosen,
my beloved with whom my soul is well pleased.
I will put my Spirit upon him, and he shall proclaim justice to the Gentiles.'

Mt. 16:27 — '. . . For the Son of man is to come with his angels in the glory of his Father, and then he will repay every man for what he has done.'

Lk. 7:16 — Fear seized them all; and they glorified God, saying, 'A great prophet has arisen among us!' and 'God has visited his people!'

Jn 6:27 — '. . . Do not labour for the food which perishes, but for the food which endures to eternal life, which the Son of man will give to you; for on him has God the Father set his seal.'

Jn 6:41,42 — The Jews then murmured at him, because he said, 'I am the bread which came down from heaven.' They said, 'Is not this Jesus, the son of Joseph, whose father and mother we know? How does he now say, "I have come down from heaven"?'

Jn 5:19-30 — Jesus said to them, 'Truly, truly, I say to you, the Son can do nothing of his own accord, but only what he sees the Father doing; for whatever he does, that the Son does likewise. For the Father loves the Son, and shows him all that he himself is doing; and greater works than these will he show him, that you may marvel. For as the Father raises the dead and gives them life, so also the Son gives life to whom he will. The Father judges no one, but has given all judgment to the Son, that all may honour the Son, even as they honour the Father. He who does not honour the Son does not honour the Father who sent him. 'Truly, truly, I say to you, he who hears my word and believes him who sent me, has eternal life; he does not come into judgment, but has passed from death to life.

'Truly, truly, I say to you, the hour is coming, and now is, when the dead will hear the voice of the Son of God, and those who hear will live. For as the Father has life in himself, so he has granted the Son also to have life in himself, and has given him authority to execute judgment, because he is the Son of man. Do not marvel at this; for the hour is coming when all who are in the tombs will hear his voice and come forth, those who have done good to the resurrection of life, and those who have done evil, to the resurrection of judgment.'

'I can do nothing on my own authority; as I hear, I judge; and my judgment is just, because I seek not my own will but the will of him who sent me.'

Jn 5:36 '. . . But the testimony which I have is greater than that of John; for the works which the Father has granted me to accomplish, these very works which I am doing, bear me witness that the Father has sent me.'

Jn 8:19 They said to him therefore, 'Where is your Father?' Jesus answered, 'You know neither me nor my Father; if you knew me, you would know my Father also.'

Jn 8:54 Jesus answered, 'If I glorify myself, my glory is nothing; it is my Father who glorifies me, of whom you say that he is your God.'

Mt. 11:25-27 At that time Jesus declared, 'I thank thee, Father, Lord of heaven and earth, that thou hast hidden these things from the wise and understanding and revealed them to babes; yea, Father, for such was thy gracious will. All things have been delivered to me by my Father; and no one knows the Son except the Father, and no one knows the Father except the Son and anyone to whom the Son chooses to reveal him.'

Jn 10:25 Jesus answered them, 'I told you, and you do not believe. The works that I do in my Father's name, they bear witness to me . . . .'

Jn 11:4 But when Jesus heard it he said, 'This illness is not unto death; it is for the glory of God, so that the Son of God may be glorified by means of it.'

Jn 11:40 Jesus said unto her, 'Did I not tell you that if you would believe you would see the glory of God?'

Jn 12:23 And Jesus answered them, 'The hour has come for the Son of man to be glorified.'

Jn 12:26-28 '. . . If any one serves me, he must follow me; and where I am, there shall my servant be also; if any one serves me, the Father will honour him.

'Now is my soul troubled. And what shall I say? "Father, save me from this hour"? No, for this purpose I have come to this hour. Father, glorify thy name.' Then a voice came from heaven, 'I have glorified it, and I will glorify it again.'

Jn 12:44-50 And Jesus cried out and said, 'He who believes in me, believes not in me, but in him who sent me. I have come as light into the world, that whoever believes in me may not remain in darkness. If any one hears my sayings and does not keep them, I do not judge him; for I did not come to judge the world but to save the world. He who rejects me and does not receive my sayings has a judge; the word that I have spoken will be his judge on the last day. For I have not spoken on my own authority; the Father who sent me has himself given me commandment what to say and what to speak. And I know that his commandment is eternal life. What I say, therefore, I say as the Father has bidden me.'

Jn 13:31,32 When he had gone out, Jesus said, 'Now is the Son of man glorified, and in him God is glorified; if God is glorified in him, God will also glorify him in himself, and glorify him at once.'

Jn 14:1 — 'Let not your hearts be troubled; believe in God, believe also in me.'

Jn 14:6-14 — Jesus said to him, 'I am the way, and the truth, and the life; no one comes to the Father, but by me. If you had known me, you would have known my Father also; henceforth you know him and have seen him.'

Philip said to him, 'Lord, show us the Father, and we shall be satisfied.' Jesus said to him, 'Have I been with you so long, and yet you do not know me, Philip? He who has seen me has seen the Father; how can you say, "Show us the Father"? Do you not believe that I am in the Father and the Father in me? The words that I say to you I do not speak on my own authority; but the Father who dwells in me does his works. Believe me that I am in the Father and the Father in me; or else believe me for the sake of the works themselves.

'Truly, truly, I say to you, he who believes in me will also do the works that I do; and greater works than these will he do, because I go to the Father. Whatever you ask in my name, I will do it, that the Father may be glorified in the Son, if you ask anything in my name, I will do it.'

Jn 14:20-24 — '. . . In that day you will know that I am in my Father, and you in me, and I in you. He who has my commandments and keeps them, he it is who loves me; and he who loves me will be loved by my Father, and I will love him and manifest myself to him.' Judas (not Iscariot) said to him, 'Lord, how is it that you will manifest yourself to us, and not to the world?' Jesus answered him, 'If a man loves me, he will keep my word, and my Father will love him, and we will come to him and make our home with him. He who does not love me does not keep my words; and the word which you hear is not mine but the Father's who sent me.'

Jn 14:28 — '. . . You heard me say to you, "I go away, and I will come to you." If you loved me, you would have rejoiced, because I go to the Father, for the Father is greater than I.'

Jn 15:1 'I am the true vine, and my Father is the vinedresser.'

Jn 15:8 '... By this is my Father glorified, that you bear much fruit, and so prove to be my disciples.'

Jn 15:15 '... No longer do I call you servants, for the servant does not know what his master is doing; but I have called you friends, for all that I have heard from my Father I have made known to you.'

Jn 16:3 '... And they will do this because they have not known the Father, nor me.'

Jn 16:10 '... of righteousness, because I go to the Father, and you will see me no more ....'

Jn 16:14,15 'He will glorify me, for he will take what is mine and declare it to you. All that the Father has is mine; therefore I said that he will take what is mine and declare it to you.'

Jn 16:26-30 '... In that day you will ask in my name; and I do not say to you that I shall pray the Father for you; for the Father himself loves you, because you have loved me and have believed that I came from the Father. I came from the Father and have come into the world; again, I am leaving the world and going to the Father.'

His disciples said, 'Ah, now you are speaking plainly and not in any figure. Now we hear that you hear all things, and need none to question you: by this we believe that you came from God.'

Jn 16:32 '... The hour is coming, indeed it has come, when you will be scattered, every man to his home, and will leave me alone; yet I am not alone, for the Father is with me.'

Jn 17:1-26 When Jesus had spoken these words, he lifted up his eyes to heaven and said, 'Father, the hour has come; glorify thy Son that the Son may glorify thee, since thou hast given him power over all flesh, to give eternal life to all whom thou hast given him. And this is eternal life, that they know thee the only true God, and Jesus Christ whom thou hast sent. I glorified thee on earth, having accomplished the work which thou gavest me to do; and now, Father, glorify thou me in thy own presence with the glory which I had with thee before the world was made.

'I have manifested thy name to the men whom thou gavest me out of the world; thine they were, and thou gavest them to me, and they have kept thy word. Now they know that everything that thou hast given me is from thee; for I have given them the words which thou gavest me, and they have received them and know in truth that I came from thee; and they have believed that thou didst send me. I am praying for them; I am not praying for the world but for those whom thou hast given me, for they are thine; all mine are thine, and thine are mine, and I am glorified in them, And now I am no more in the world, but they are in the world, and I am coming to thee. Holy Father, keep them in thy name, which thou hast given me, that they may be one, even as we are one. While I was with them, I kept them in thy name, which thou hast given me; I have guarded them, and none of them is lost but the son of perdition, that the scripture might be fulfilled. But now I am coming to thee; and these things I speak in the world, that they may have my joy fulfilled in themselves. I have given them thy word; and the world has hated them because they are not of the world, even as I am not of the world. I do not pray that thou shouldst take them out of the world, but that thou shouldst keep them from the evil one. They are not of the world, even as I am not of the world. Sanctify them in truth; thy word is truth. As thou didst send me into the world, so I have sent them into the world. And for their sake I consecrate myself, that they also may be consecrated in truth.

'I do not pray for these only, but also for those who believe in me through their word that they may all be one; even as thou, Father, art in me and I in thee, that they also may be in us, so that the world may believe that thou hast sent me. The glory which thou has given me I have given to them, that they may be one even as we are one, I in thee and thee in me, that they may become perfectly one, so that the world may know that thou hast sent me and hast loved me. Father, I desire that they also, whom thou hast given me, may be with me where I am, to behold my glory which thou hast given me in thy love for me before the foundation of the world. O righteous Father, the world has not known thee, but I have known thee; and these know that thou hast sent me. I made known to them thy name, and I will make it known, that the love with which thou hast loved me may be in them, and I in them.'

Jn 21:18,19 'Truly, truly, I say to you, when you were young, you girded yourself and walked where you would, but when you are old, you will stretch out your hands, and another will gird you and carry you where you do not wish to go.' And after this he said to him, 'Follow me.'

v. Jesus does the Father's Will

Lk. 2:49 And he said to them, 'How is it that you sought me? Did you not know that I must be in my Father's house?'

Mt. 4:4 But he answered, 'It is written, "Man shall not live by bread alone, but by every word that proceeds from the mouth of God." '

Jn 4:34 Jesus said to them, 'My food is to do the will of him who sent me, and to accomplish his work.'

Jn 6:38 '. . . For I have come down from heaven, not to do my own will, but the will of him who sent me . . . .'

Jn 5:19 Jesus said to them 'Truly, truly, I say to you, the Son can do nothing of his own accord, but only what he sees the Father doing; for whatever he does, that the Son does likewise.'

Jn 5:30 'I can do nothing on my own authority; as I hear, I judge; and my judgment is just, because I seek not my own will but the will of him who sent me.'

Jn 8:28,29 So Jesus said, 'When you have lifted up the Son of man, then you will know that I am he, and that I do nothing on my own authority but speak thus as the Father taught me. And he who sent me is with me; he has not left me alone, for I always do what is pleasing to him.'

Jn 9:4 '. . . We must work the works of him who sent me, while it is day; night comes, when no one can work.'

Jn 12:49,50	'. . . For I have not spoken on my own authority; the Father who sent me has himself given me commandment what to say and what to speak. And I know that his commandment is eternal life. What I say, therefore, I say as the Father has bidden me.'
Jn 14:23,24	Jesus answered him, 'If a man loves me, he will keep my word, and my Father will love him, and we will come to him and make our home with him. He who does not love me does not keep my words; and the word which you hear is not mine but the Father's who sent me.'
Jn 14:31	'. . . but I do as the Father has commanded me, so that the world may know that I love the Father. Rise, let us go hence.'
Jn 15:10	'. . . If you keep my commandments, you will abide in my love, just as I have kept my Father's commandments and abide in his love.'
Mt. 26:39	And going a little farther he fell on his face and prayed, 'My Father, if it be possible, let this cup pass from me; nevertheless, not as I will, but as thou wilt.'
Mt. 26:42	Again, for the second time, he went away and prayed, 'My Father, if this cannot pass unless I drink it, thy will be done.'
Jn 19:30	When Jesus had received the vinegar, he said, 'it is finished'; and he bowed his head and gave up his spirit.
Lk. 23:46	Then Jesus, crying with a loud voice, said, 'Father, into thy hands I commit my spirit!'

vi. Jesus and the Spirit

Lk. 1:35	And the angel said to her, 'The Holy Spirit will come upon you, and the power of the Most High will overshadow you; therefore the child to be born will be called holy, the Son of God.
Lk. 1:67	And his father Zechariah was filled with the Holy Spirit, and prophesied . . .
Mt. 1:18–20	Now the birth of Jesus Christ took place in this way. When his mother Mary had been betrothed to Joseph, before they came together she was found to be with

child of the Holy Spirit; and her husband Joseph, being a just man and unwilling to put her to shame, resolved to send her away quietly. But as he considered this, behold, an angel of the Lord appeared to him in a dream, saying, 'Joseph, son of David, do not fear to take Mary your wife, for that which is conceived in her is of the Holy Spirit . . . .'

Lk. 2:27,28 — And inspired by the Spirit he came into the temple; and when the parents brought in the child Jesus, to do for him according to the custom of the law, he took him up in his arms and blessed God . . . .

Mt. 3:11 — 'I baptize you with water for repentance, but he who is coming after me is mightier than I, whose sandals I am not worthy to carry; he will baptize you with the Holy Spirit and with fire.'

Lk. 4:1 — And Jesus, full of the Holy Spirit, returned from the Jordan, and was led by the Spirit . . . .

Jn 1:32,33 — And John bore witness, 'I saw the Spirit descend as a dove from heaven, and it remained on him.'

Jn 3:5,6 — Jesus answered, 'Truly, truly, I say to you, unless one is born of water and the Spirit, he cannot enter the kingdom of God. That which is born of the flesh is flesh, and that which is born of the Spirit is spirit.'

Jn 3:8 — '. . . The wind blows where it wills, and you hear the sound of it, but you do not know whence it comes or whither it goes; so it is with every one who is born of the Spirit.'

Jn 3:34 — For he whom God has sent utters the words of God, for it is not by measure that he gives the Spirit . . . .'

Lk. 4:18 — 'The Spirit of the Lord is upon me, because he has anointed me to preach the good news to the poor. He has sent me to proclaim release to the captives and recovering of sight to the blind, to set at liberty those who are oppressed . . . .'

Mt. 12:18 — 'Behold my servant whom I have chosen, my beloved with whom my soul is well pleased. I will put my Spirit upon him, and he shall proclaim justice to the Gentiles.'

Jn 7:38,39
'... He who believes in me, as the scripture has said, "Out of his heart shall flow rivers of living water."'

Now this he said about the Spirit, which those who believed in him were to receive; for as yet the Spirit had not been given, because Jesus was not yet glorified.

Lk. 10:21
In that same hour he rejoiced in the Holy Spirit and said, 'I thank thee, Father, Lord of heaven and earth, that thou hast hidden these things from the wise and understanding and revealed them to babes; yea, Father, for such was thy gracious will.'

Mk 3:29
'... but whoever blasphemes against the Holy Spirit never has forgiveness, but is guilty of an eternal sin'

Lk. 12:12
'... for the Holy Spirit will teach you in that very hour what you ought to say.'

Jn 14:15-17
'If you love me, you will keep my commandments. And I will pray the Father, and he will give you another Counsellor, to be with you for ever, even the Spirit of truth, whom the world cannot receive, because if neither sees him nor knows him; you know him, for he dwells with you, and will be in you.'

Jn 14:26
'... But the Counsellor, the Holy Spirit, whom the Father will send in my name, he will teach you all things, and bring to you remembrance all that I have said to you.'

Jn 15:26
'... But when the Counsellor comes, who I shall send to you from the Father, even the Spirit of truth, who proceeds from the Father, he will bear witness to me ....'

Jn 16:7-15
'... Nevertheless I tell you the truth; it is to your advantage that I go away, for if I do not go away, the Counsellor will not come to you; but if I go, I will send him to you. And when he comes, he will convince the world of sin and of righteousness and of judgment: of sin, because they do not believe in me; of righteousness, because I go to the Father, and you will see me no more; of judgment, because the ruler of this world is judged.

'I have yet many things to say to you, but you cannot bear them now. When the Spirit of truth comes, he will guide you into all the truth; for he will not speak on his own authority, but whatever he hears he will speak, and he will declare to you the things that are to come. He will glorify me, for he will take what is mine and declare it to you. All that the Father has is mine; therefore I said that he will take what is mine and declare it to you.'

Jn 20:22 — And when he had said this, he breathed on them, and said to them, 'Receive the Holy Spirit.'

Mt. 28:19 — 'Go therefore and make disciples of all nations, baptizing them in the name of the Father and of the Son and of the Holy Spirit . . . .'

Lk. 24:44 — Then he said to them, 'These are my words which I spoke to you, while I was still with you, that everything written about me in the law of Moses and the prophets and the psalms must be fulfilled.'

vii. Omnipotence

Jn 1:3 — . . . all things were made through him, and without him was not anything made that was made.

Jn 1:10 — He was in the world, and the world was made through him, yet the world knew him not.

Lk. 1:37 — '. . . For with God nothing will be impossible.'

Lk. 12:28 — '. . . But if God so clothes the grass which is alive in the field today and tomorrow is thrown into the oven, how much more will he clothe you, O men of little faith.'

Mt. 28:18 — And Jesus came and said to them, 'All authority in heaven and on earth has been given to me.'

5. Jesus: His Office

i. Jesus' office in general

Jn 1:11-14 He came to his own home, and his own people received him not. But to all who received him, who believed in his name, he gave power to become children of God; who were born, not of blood nor of the will of the flesh nor of the will of man, but of God.

And the Word became flesh and dwelt among us, full of grace and truth; we have beheld his glory, glory as of the only Son from the Father.

Jn 1:17,18 For the law was given through Moses; grace and truth came through Jesus Christ. No one has ever seen God; the only Son, who is in the bosom of the Father, he has made him known.

Lk. 1:32 He will be great, and will be called the Son of the Most High, and the Lord God will give to him the throne of his father David,

Mt. 1:21 '. . . she will bear a son, and you shall call his name Jesus, for he will save the people from their sins.'

Lk. 2:11 '. . . for to you is born this day in the city of David a Saviour, who is Christ the Lord.'

Lk. 2:34 . . . and Simeon blessed them and said to Mary his mother, 'Behold, this child is set for the fall and rising of many in Israel, and for a sign that is spoken against . . .'

Lk. 3:6 '. . . and all flesh shall see the salvation of God.'

Lk. 3:16,17 John answered them all, 'I baptise you with water; but he who is mightier than I is coming, the thong of whose sandals I am not worthy to untie; he will baptise you with the Holy Spirit and with fire. His winnowing fork is in his hand, to clear his threshing floor, and to gather the wheat into his granary, but the chaff he will burn with unquenchable fire.'

Jn 1:29 The next day he saw Jesus coming towards him, and said, 'Behold, the Lamb of God, who takes away the sin of the world.'

Jn 3:16-18 — For God so loved the world that he gave his only Son, that whoever believes in him should not perish but have eternal life. For God sent the Son into the world, not to condemn the world, but that the world might be saved through him. He who believes in him is not condemned; he who does not believe is condemned already, because he has not believed in the name of the only Son of God.

Jn 4:34 — Jesus said to them, 'My food is to do the will of him who sent me, and to accomplish his work.'

Mk 1:14,15 — Now after John was arrested, Jesus came into Galilee, preaching the gospel of God, and saying, 'The time is fulfilled, and the kingdom of God is at hand; repent, and believe in the gospel.'

Lk. 4:17-21 — . . . and there was given to him the book of the prophet Isaiah. He opened the book and found the place where it was written,

> 'The Spirit of the Lord is upon me,
> because he has anointed me to preach good news to the poor.
> He sent me to proclaim release to the captives
> and recovering of sight to the blind,
> to set at liberty those who are oppressed,
> to proclaim the acceptable year of the Lord.'

And he closed the book and gave it back to the attendant, and sat down; and the eyes of all in the synagogue were fixed on him. And he began to say to them, 'Today this scripture has been fulfilled in your hearing.'

Mt. 5:17 — 'Think not that I have come to abolish the law and the prophets; I have come not to abolish them but to fulfil them.'

Jn 6:38-40 — 'For I have come down from heaven, not to do my own will, but the will of him who sent me, that I should lose nothing of all that he has given me, but raise it up at the last day. For this is the will of my Father, that everyone who sees the Son and believes in him should have eternal life; and I will raise him up at the last day.'

Mt. 15:24 — He answered, 'I was sent only to the lost sheep of the house of Israel.'

Mt. 18:11	'For the Son of man came to save the lost.'
Lk. 9:56	'. . . you do not know what manner of spirit you are of; for the Son of man came not to destroy men's lives but to save them.'
Lk. 12:49-51	'I came to cast fire upon the earth; and would that it were already kindled! I have a baptism to be baptized with; and how I am constrained until it is accomplished! Do you think that I have come to give peace on earth? No, I tell you, but rather division . . . .'
Mk 10:45	'For the Son of man also came not to be served but to serve, and to give his life as a ransom for many.'
Jn 18:37	Pilate said to him, 'So you are a king?' Jesus answered, 'You say that I am a king. For this I was born, and for this I have come into the world, to bear witness to the truth. Every one who is of the truth hears my voice.'
Lk. 24:44-48	Then he said to them, 'These are my words which I spoke to you, while I was still with you, that everything written about me in the law of Moses and the prophets and the psalms must be fulfilled.' Then he opened their minds to understand the scriptures, and said to them, 'Thus it is written, that the Christ should suffer and on the third day rise from the dead, and that repentance and forgiveness of sins should be preached in his name to all nations, beginning from Jerusalem. You are witnesses to these things.'
Mt. 28:18-20	And Jesus came and said to them, 'All authority in heaven and on earth has been given to me. Go therefore and make disciples of all nations, baptizing them in the name of the Father and of the Son and of the Holy Spirit, teaching them to observe all that I have commanded you; and lo, I am with you always, to the close of the age.'

ii. Jesus is Prophet and Teacher

Jn 3:2	This man came to Jesus by night and said to him, 'Rabbi, we know that you are a teacher come from God; for no one can do these signs that you do, unless God is with him.'

Jn 3:11,12	'Truly, truly, I say to you, we speak of what we know, and bear witness to what we have seen; but you do not receive our testimony. If I have told you earthly things and you do not believe, how can you believe if I tell you heavenly things?'
Jn 3:32-34	He bears witness to what he has seen and heard, yet no one receives his testimony; he who receives his testimony sets his seal to this, that God is true. For he whom God has sent utters the words of God, for it is not by measure that he gives the Spirit;
Jn 4:43,44	After the two days he departed to Galilee. For Jesus himself testified that a prophet has no honour in his own country.
Mk 1:38,39	And he said to them, 'Let us go on to the next town, that I may preach there also; for that is why I came out.' And he went throughout all Galilee, preaching in their synagogues and casting out demons.
Mt. 5:17	'. . . Think not that I have come to abolish the law and the prophets, I have come not to abolish them but to fulfil them.'
Mk 6:4	And Jesus said to them, 'A prophet is not without honour, except in his own country and among his own kin, and in his own house.'
Jn 6:14	When the people saw the sign which he had done, they said, 'This is indeed the prophet who is to come into the world.'
Jn 6:64	'But there are some of you who do not believe.' For Jesus knew from the first who those were that did not believe, and who it was that should betray him.
Jn 7:40-42	When they heard these words, some of the people said, 'This is really the prophet.' Others said, 'This is the Christ.' But some said, 'Is the Christ to come from Galilee? Has not the scripture said that the Christ is descended from David, and comes from Bethlehem, the village where David was?'
Jn 8:31,32	Jesus then said to the Jews who had believed in him, 'If you continue in my word, you are truly my disciples, and

you will know the truth, and the truth will make you free.'

Jn 8:38	'I speak of what I have seen with my Father, and you do what you have heard from your father.'
Lk. 10:21	In that same hour he rejoiced in the Holy Spirit and said, 'I thank thee, Father, Lord of heaven and earth, that thou hast hidden these things from the wise and understanding and revealed them to babes; yea, Father, for such was thy gracious will.'
Jn 12:49,50	'For I have not spoken on my own authority; the Father who sent me has himself given me commandment what to say and what to speak. And I know that his commandment is eternal life. What I say, therefore, I say as the Father has bidden me.'
Mk 13:31	'Heaven and earth will pass away, but my words will not pass away.'
Lk. 24:19	And he said to them, 'What things?' And they said to him, 'Concerning Jesus of Nazareth, who was a prophet mighty in deed and word before God and all the people . . . .'
Mt. 28:18-20	And Jesus came and said to them, 'All authority in heaven and on earth has been given to me. Go therefore and make disciples of all nations, baptizing them in the name of the Father and of the Son and of the Holy Spirit, teaching them to observe all that I have commanded you; and lo, I am with you always, to the close of the age.'

iii. Forecasts of his Passion

Jn 2:18,19	The Jews then said to him, 'What sign have you to show us for doing this?' Jesus answered them 'Destroy this temple, and in three days I will raise it up.'
Mt. 16:21	From that time Jesus began to show his disciples that he must go to Jerusalem and suffer many things from the elders and chief priests and scribes, and be killed, and on the third day be raised.

Mk 9:11,12	And they asked him, 'Why do the scribes say that first Elijah must come?' And he said to them 'Elijah does come first to restore all things; and how is it written of the Son of man, that he should suffer many things and be treated with contempt?'
Mk 9:30-32	They went on from there and passed through Galilee. And he would not have anyone know it; for he was teaching his disciples, saying to them, 'The Son of man will be delivered into the hands of men, and they will kill him; and when he is killed, after three days he will rise.' But they did not understand the saying, and they were afraid to ask him.
Jn 8:28,29	So Jesus said, 'When you have lifted up the Son of man, then you will know that I am he, and that I do not speak on my own authority but speak thus as the Father taught me. And he who sent me is with me; he has not left me alone, for I always do what is pleasing to him.'
Jn 11:50-52	'. . . you do not understand that it is expedient for you that one man should die for the people, and that the whole nation should not perish.' He did not say this of his own accord, but being high priest that year he prophesied that Jesus should die for the nation, and not for the nation only, but to gather into one the children of God who are scattered abroad.
Jn 12:32,33	'. . . and I, when I am lifted up from the earth, will draw all men to myself.' He said this to show by what death he was to die.
Mt. 26:2	'You know that after two days the Passover is coming, and the Son of man will be delivered up to be crucified.'
Mt. 26:12	'In pouring this ointment on my body she has done it to prepare me for burial.'
Mk 14:18	And as they were at table eating, Jesus said, 'Truly, I say to you, one of you will betray me, one who is eating with me.'
Mk 14:27	And Jesus said to them, 'You will all fall away; for it is written, "I will strike the shepherd, and the sheep will be scattered."'

iv. His Resurrection

Jn 2:19	Jesus answered them 'Destroy this temple, and in three days I will raise it up.'
Mt. 16:21	From that time Jesus began to show his disciples that he must go to Jerusalem and suffer many things from the elders and the chief priests and the scribes, and be killed, and on the third day be raised.
Mk 9:9,10	And as they were coming down the mountain, he charged them to tell no one what they had seen, until the Son of man should have risen from the dead. So they kept the matter to themselves, questioning what the rising from the dead meant.
Mk 9:30-32	They went on from there and passed through Galilee. And he would not have any one know it; for he was teaching his disciples, saying to them, 'The Son of man will be delivered into the hands of men, and they will kill him; and when he is killed, after three days he will rise.' But they did not understand the saying, and they were afraid to ask him.
Mt. 12:40	'For as Jonah was three days and three nights in the belly of a whale, so will the Son of man be three days and three nights in the heart of the earth.'
Mk 14:28	'But after I am raised up, I will go before you to Galilee.'
Mt. 26:61	. . . and said, 'This fellow said, "I am able to destroy the temple of God, and to build it in three days."'
Mt. 27:62-64	Next day, that is, after the day of Preparation, the chief priests and the Pharisees gathered before Pilate and said, 'Sir, we remember how that imposter said, while he was still alive, "After three days I will rise again." Therefore order the sepulchre to be made secure until the third day, lest his disciples go and steal him away, and tell the people "He is risen from the dead", and the last fraud will be worse than the first.'
Jn 20:2	So she ran, and went to Simon Peter and the other disciple, the one whom Jesus loved, and said to them, 'They have taken the Lord out of the tomb, and we do not know where they have laid him.'

Mt. 28:6,7 'He is not here; for he has risen, as he said. Come, see the place where he lay. Then go quickly and tell his disciples that he has risen from the dead, and behold, he is going before you to Galilee; there you will see him. Lo, I have told you.'

Lk. 24:9-11 . . . and returning from the tomb they told all this to the eleven and to all the rest. Now it was Mary Magdalene and Joanna and Mary the mother of James and the other women with them who told this to the apostles; but these words seemed to them an idle tale, and they did not believe them.

Jn 20:6-9 Then Simon Peter came, following him, and went into the tomb; he saw the linen cloths lying there, and the napkin which had been on his head, not lying with the linen cloths but rolled up in a place by itself. Then the other disciple, who reached the tomb first, also went in, and he saw and believed; for as yet they did not know the scripture, that he must rise from the dead.

Jn 20:14-18 . . . saying this, she turned round and saw Jesus standing, but she did not know that it was Jesus. Jesus said to her, 'Woman, why are you weeping? Whom do you seek?' Supposing him to be the gardener, she said to him, 'Sir, if you have carried him away, tell me where you have laid him, and I will take him away.' Jesus said to her, 'Mary'. She turned and said to him in Hebrew, 'Rabboni!' (which means Teacher). Jesus said to her, 'Do not hold me, for I have not yet ascended to the Father; but go to my brethren and say to them, I am ascending to my Father and your Father, to my God and your God.' Mary Magdalene went and said to the disciples, 'I have seen the Lord'; and she told them that he had said these things to her.

Mt. 28:12-15 And when they had assembled with the elders and taken counsel, they gave a sum of money to the soldiers and said, 'Tell the people, "His disciples came by night and stole him away while we were asleep," And if this comes to the governor's ears, we will satisfy him and keep you out of trouble.' So they took the money and did as they were directed; and this story has been spread among the Jews to this day.

Lk. 24:39-43 'See my hands and my feet, that it is I myself; handle me, and see; for a spirit has not flesh and bones as you see that I have.' And when he had said this, he showed them his hands and his feet. And while they still disbelieved for joy, and wondered, he said to them, 'Have you anything here to eat?' They gave him a piece of broiled fish, and he took it and ate before them.

Jn 20:24-29 Now Thomas, one of the twelve, called the Twin, was not with them when Jesus came. So the other disciples told him, 'We have seen the Lord.' But he said to them, 'Unless I see in his hands the print of the nails, and place my finger in the mark of the nails, and place my hand in his side, I will not believe.' Eight days later, his disciples were again in the house, and Thomas was with them. The doors were shut, but Jesus came and stood among them, and said, 'Peace be with you.' Then he said to Thomas, 'Put your finger here and see my hands; and put your hand and place it in my side; do not be faithless, but believing.' Thomas answered him, 'My Lord and my God!' Jesus said to him, 'Have you believed because you have seen me? Blessed are those who have not seen and yet believe.'

Jn 21:12-19 Jesus said to them, 'Come and have breakfast.' Now none of the disciples dared ask him, 'Who are you?' They knew it was the Lord. Jesus came and took the bread and gave it to them, and so with the fish. This was now the third time that Jesus was revealed to the disciples after he was raised from the dead.

Mt. 28:16-20 Now the eleven disciples went to Galilee, to the mountain to which Jesus had directed them. And when they saw him they worshipped him; but some doubted. And Jesus came and said to them, 'All authority in heaven and on earth has been given to me. Go therefore and make disciples of all nations, baptizing them in the name of the Father and of the Son and of the Holy Spirit, teaching them to observe all that I have commanded you; and lo, I am with you always, to the close of the age.'

Lk. 24:44-52 Then he said to them, 'These are my words which I spoke to you, while I was still with you, that everything written about me in the law of Moses and the prophets and the psalms must be fulfilled.' Then he opened their minds to understand the scriptures, and said to them, 'Thus it is written, that the Christ should suffer and on the third day rise from the dead, and that repentance and forgiveness of sins should be preached in his name to all nations, beginning from Jerusalem. You are witnesses of these things. And behold, I send the promise of my Father upon you; but stay in the city, until you are clothed with power from on high. Then he led them out as far as Bethany, and lifting up his hands he blessed them. While he blessed them, he parted from them, and was carried up into heaven. And they worshipped him, and returned to Jerusalem with great joy.

v. Jesus will return

Mt. 16:27 'For the Son of man is to come with his angels in the glory of his Father, and then he will repay every man for what he has done.'

Lk. 12:40 'You must be ready; for the Son of man is coming at an hour you do not expect.'

Lk. 12:46 '... The master of that servant will come on a day when he does not expect him and at an hour he does not know, and will punish him, and put him with the unfaithful.'

Lk. 17:24 'For as the lightning flashes and lights up the sky from one side to the other, so will the Son of man be in his day.'

Lk. 21:27 'And then they will see the Son of man coming in a cloud with power and great glory.'

Lk. 21:31 'So also, when you see these things taking place, you will know that the kingdom of God is near ....'

Mt. 25:31 'When the Son of man comes in his glory, and all the angels with him, then he will sit on his glorious throne.'

Lk. 22:69-71 'But from now on the Son of man shall be seated at the right hand of the power of God.' And they all said, 'Are you the Son of God, then?' and he said to them, 'You say that I am.' And they said, 'What further testimony do we need? We have heard it from his own lips.'

See also: 3. Our Saviour
6. Jesus: The King

6. Jesus: The King

i. Jesus and Kingship

Lk. 1:32,33 'He will be great, and will be called the Son of the Most High;
And the Lord God will give to him the throne of his father David,
And he will reign over the house of Jacob for ever;
and of his kingdom there will be no end.'

Mt. 2:2 'Where is he who has been born king of the Jews? For we have seen his star in the East, and have come to worship him.'

Mt. 2:6 'And you, O Bethlehem, in the land of Judah,
are by no means least among the rulers of Judah;
for from you shall come a ruler
who will govern my people Israel.'

Jn 1:49 Nathanael answered him, 'Rabbi, you are the Son of God! You are the King of Israel.'

Jn 3:3 Jesus answered him, 'Truly, truly, I say to you, unless one is born anew he cannot see the kingdom of God.'

Mt. 5:3 'Blessed are the poor in spirit, for theirs is the kingdom of heaven.'

Mt. 5:10 'Blessed are those who are persecuted for righteousness' sake, for theirs is the kingdom of heaven.'

Mt. 5:35 'Do not swear at all, either by heaven, for it is the throne of God, or by the earth, for it is his footstool, or by Jerusalem, for it is the city of the great King.'

Jn 6:15 Perceiving that they were about to come and take him by force to make him king, Jesus withdrew again to the hills by himself.

Jn 7:42 'Has not the scripture said that the Christ is descended from David, and comes from Bethlehem, the village where David was?'

Mt. 21:4,5 This took place to fulfil what was spoken by the prophet, saying, 'Tell the daughter of Zion, Behold your king is coming to you, humble, and mounted on an ass, and on a colt, the foal of an ass.'

Mt. 25:31	'When the Son of man comes in his glory, and all the angels with him, then he will sit on his glorious throne.'
Mt. 25:40	And the King will answer them, 'Truly I say to you, as you did it to one of the least of these my brethren, you did it to me.'
Lk. 22:29,30	'. . . as my Father appointed a kingdom for me, so do I appoint for you that you may eat and drink at my table in my kingdom, and sit on thrones judging the twelve tribes of Israel.'
Mt. 26:29	'I tell you I shall not drink again of this fruit of the vine until the day when I drink it new with you in my Father's kingdom.'
Jn 18:36,37	Jesus answered, 'My kingship is not of this world; if my kingship were of this world, my servants would fight, that I might not be handed over to the Jews; but my kingship is not from the world.' Pilate said to him, 'So you are a king?' Jesus answered, 'You say that I am a king. For this was I born, and for this I have come into the world, to bear witness to the truth. Every one who is of the truth hears my voice.'
Mk 15:9	And he answered them, 'Do you want me to release for you the King of the Jews?'
Jn 18:39,40	'But you have a custom that I should release for you one man at the Passover; will you have me release for you the King of the Jews?' They cried out again, 'Not this man but Barabbas!' Now Barabbas was a robber.
Mk 15:12,13	And Pilate again said to them, 'Then what shall I do with the man whom you call the King of the Jews?' And they cried out again, 'Crucify him.'
Jn 19:2,3	And the soldiers plaited a crown of thorns, and put it on his head, and arraying him in a purple robe, they came up to him, saying, 'Hail, King of the Jews!' And struck him with their hands.
Jn 19:12	Upon this Pilate sought to release him, but the Jews cried out, 'If you release this man, you are not Caesar's friend; every one who makes himself a king sets himself against Caesar.'

Jn 19:14,15 Now it was the day of Preparation of the Passover, it was about the sixth hour. He said to the Jews, 'Here is your King!' They cried out, 'Away with him, away with him, crucify him.' Pilate said to them, 'Shall I crucify your King?' The Chief Priests answered, 'We have no king but Caesar.'

Jn 19:19-22 Pilate wrote a title and put it on the cross; it read, 'Jesus of Nazareth, King of the Jews.' Many of the Jews read this title, for the place where Jesus was crucified was near the city; and it was written in Hebrew, in Latin, and in Greek. The chief priests of the Jews said to Pilate, 'Do not write "King of the Jews", but "This man said, I am King of the Jews." Pilate answered, 'What I have written I have written.'

Mt. 27:42 'He saved others; he cannot save himself. He is the King of Israel; let him come down now from the cross, and we will believe him.'

Lk. 23:42,43 And he said, 'Jesus, remember me when you come in your kingly power.' And he said to him, 'Truly, I say to you, today you will be with me in Paradise.'

ii. The Kingdom

Mt. 4:23 And he went about all Galilee, teaching in their synagogues and preaching the gospel of the kingdom and healing every kind of disease and every infirmity among the people.

Mt. 5:3 'Blessed are the poor in spirit, for theirs is the kingdom of heaven.'

Mt. 5:10 'Blessed are those who are persecuted for righteousness' sake, for theirs is the kingdom of heaven.'

Mt. 7:21 'Not every one who says to me, "Lord, Lord," shall enter the kingdom of heaven, but he who does the will of my Father who is in heaven.'

Lk. 16:16 'The law and the prophets were until John; since then the good news of the kingdom of God is preached, and every one enters it violently.'

Mt. 11:11,12 — 'Truly, I say to you, among those born of women there has risen no one greater than John the Baptist, yet he who is least in the kingdom of heaven is greater than he. From the days of John the Baptist until now the kingdom of heaven has suffered violence, and men of violence take it by force.'

Lk. 8:1 — Soon afterwards he went on through cities and villages, preaching and bringing the good news of the kingdom of God.

Mk 4:11 — And he said to them, 'To you has been given the secret of the kingdom of God, but to those outside everything is in parables.'

Mt. 13:19 — 'When any one hears the word of the kingdom and does not understand it, the evil one comes and snatches away what is sown in his heart; this is what was sown along the path.'

Mk 4:26,27 — And he said, 'The kingdom of God is as if a man should scatter seed upon the ground, and should sleep and rise night and day, and the seed should sprout and grow, he knows not how.'

Mt. 13:24,25 — Another parable he put before them, saying, 'The kingdom of heaven may be compared to a man who sowed good seed in his field; but while men were sleeping, his enemy came and sowed weeds among the wheat, and went away.'

Lk. 13:18,19 — He said therefore, 'What is the kingdom of God like? And to what shall I compare it? It is like a grain of mustard seed which a man took and sowed in his garden; and it grew and became a tree, and the birds of the air made nests in its branches.'

Mt. 13:33 — 'The kingdom of heaven is like leaven which a woman took and hid in three measures of meal, till it was all leavened.'

Mt. 13:44 — 'The kingdom of heaven is like treasure hidden in a field, which a man found and covered up; then in his joy he goes and sells all that he has and buys that field.'

Mt. 13:47 — 'Again, the kingdom of heaven is like a net which was thrown into the sea and gathered fish of every kind . . . .'

Mt. 9:35	And Jesus went about all the cities and villages, teaching in their synagogues and preaching the gospel of the kingdom, and healing every disease and every infirmity.
Lk. 9:2	. . . and he sent them out to preach the kingdom of God and to heal.
Lk. 9:27	'But I tell you truly, there are some standing here who will not taste death before they see the kingdom of God.'
Mt. 18:3,4	'Truly, I say to you, unless you turn and become like children you will never enter the kingdom of heaven. Whoever humbles himself like this child, he is the greatest in the kingdom of heaven.'
Mk 9:47	'And if your eye causes you to sin, pluck it out; it is better for you to enter the kingdom of God with one eye than with two eyes to be thrown into hell.'
Mt. 18:23	'Therefore the kingdom of heaven may be compared to a king who wished to settle accounts with his servants.'
Lk. 10:8-11	'Whenever you enter a town and they receive you, eat what is set before you; heal the sick in it and say to them, "The kingdom of God has come near to you." But whenever you enter a town and they do not receive you, go into its streets and say, "Even the dust of your town that clings to our feet, we wipe off against you; nevertheless know this, that the kingdom of God has come near." '
Mk 12:34	And when Jesus saw that he answered wisely, he said to him, 'You are not far from the kingdom of God.' And after that no one dared to ask him any questions.
Mt. 6:10	Thy kingdom come, Thy will be done, On earth as it is in heaven.
Mt. 12:28	'But if it is by the Spirit of God that I cast out demons, then the kingdom of God has come upon you.'
Lk. 12:32	'Fear not, little flock, for it is your Father's good pleasure to give you the kingdom.'
Mt. 8:11,12	'I tell you, many will come from east and west and sit at table with Abraham, Isaac, and Jacob in the kingdom of

Heaven, while the sons of the kingdom will be thrown into the outer darkness; there men will weep and gnash their teeth.'

Mt. 22:2 — 'The kingdom of heaven may be compared to a king who gave a marriage feast for his son.'

Mt. 5:19 — 'Whoever then relaxes one of the least of these commandments and teaches men so, shall be called least in the kingdom of heaven; but he who does them and teaches them shall be called great in the kingdom of heaven.'

Lk. 17:20,21 — Being asked by the Pharisees when the kingdom of God was coming, he answered them, 'The kingdom of God is not coming with signs to be observed; nor will they say, "Lo, here it is." or "There" for behold the kingdom of God is in the midst of you.'

Lk. 18:16,17 — But Jesus called them to him, saying, 'Let the children come to me and do not hinder them; for to such belongs the kingdom of God. Truly, I say to you, whoever does not receive the kingdom of God like a child shall not enter it.'

Mk 10:23-25 — And Jesus looked around and said to his disciples, 'How hard it is for those who have riches to enter the kingdom of God.' And the disciples were amazed at his words. But Jesus said to them again, 'Children, how hard it is for those who trust in riches to enter the kingdom of God! It is easier for a camel to go through the eye of a needle than for a rich man to enter the kingdom of God.'

Mt. 20:1 — 'For the kingdom of heaven is like a householder who went out early in the morning to hire labourers for his vineyard.'

Mt. 20:21 — And he said to her, 'What do you want,' She said to him, 'Command that these two sons of mine may sit, one at your right hand and one at your left, in your kingdom.'

Lk. 19:11,12 — As they heard these things, he proceeded to tell them a parable, because he was near to Jerusalem, and because they supposed that the kingdom of God was to appear immediately. He said therefore, 'A nobleman went into a far country to receive kingly power and then return.'

Lk. 19:27	'But as for those enemies of mine, who did not want me to reign over them, bring them here and slay them before me.'
Mt. 21:31	'Which of the two did the will of his father?' They said, 'The first.' Jesus said to them, 'Truly, I say to you, the tax collectors and the harlots go into the kingdom of God before you.'
Mt. 24:14	'And this gospel of the kingdom will be preached throughout the whole world, as a testimony to all nations; and then the end will come.'
Lk. 21:31	'So also, when you see these things taking place, you will know that the kingdom of God is near.'
Mt. 25:1	'Then the kingdom of heaven shall be compared to ten maidens who took their lamps and went to meet the bridegroom.'
Lk. 23:50,51	Now there was a man named Joseph from the Jewish town of Arimathea. He was a member of the council, a good and righteous man, who had not consented to their purpose and deed, and he was looking for the kingdom of God.

7. Jesus: Gifts and Signs

i. Jesus and Life, Sonship

Jn 1:4	In him was life, and the life was the light of men.
Jn 1:12,13	But to all who received him, who believed in his name, he gave power to become children of God, who were born, not of blood nor of the will of the flesh nor of the will of man, but of God.
Jn 1:16	And from his fullness have we all received, grace upon grace.
Jn 3:3-8	Jesus answered him, 'Truly, truly, I say to you, unless one is born anew, he cannot see the kingdom of God.' Nicodemus said to him, 'How can a man be born when he is old? Can he enter a second time into his mother's womb and be born?' Jesus answered, 'Truly, truly, I say to you, unless one is born of water and the Spirit, he cannot enter the kingdom of God. That which is born of the flesh is flesh, and that which is born of the Spirit is spirit. Do not marvel that I say to you, "You must be born anew!" The wind blows where it wills, and you hear the sound of it, but you do not know whence it comes or whither it goes; so it is with every one who is born of the Spirit.'
Jn 3:15-16	'And as Moses lifted up the serpent in the wilderness, so must the Son of man be lifted up, that whoever believes in him may have eternal life.' For God so loved the world that he gave his only Son, that whoever believes in him should not perish but have eternal life.
Jn 4:14	'. . . but whoever drinks of the water that I shall give him will never thirst; the water that I shall give him will become like a spring of water welling up to eternal life.'
Lk. 6:35	'But love your enemies, and do good, and lend, expecting nothing in return; and your reward will be great, and you will be sons of the Most High; for he is kind to the ungrateful and the selfish.'

Jn 6:27 'Do not labour for the food which perishes, but for the food which endures to eternal life, which the Son of man will give to you; for on him has God the father set his seal.'

Jn 6:32-35 Jesus then said to them, 'Truly, truly, I say to you, it was not Moses who gave you bread from heaven; my Father gives you the true bread from heaven. For the bread of God is that which comes down from heaven, and gives life to the world.' They said to him, 'Lord, give us this bread always.' Jesus said to them, 'I am the bread of life; he who comes to me shall not hunger, and he who believes in me shall never thirst.'

Jn 6:40-41 'For this is the will of my Father, that everyone who sees the Son and believes in him should have eternal life; and I will raise him up at the last day.' The Jews then murmured at him, because he said, 'I am the bread which came down from heaven.'

Jn 6:44 'No one can come to me unless the Father who sent me draws him; and I will raise him up at the last day.'

Jn 6:47-59 'Truly, truly, I say to you, he who believes has eternal life. I am the bread of life. Your fathers ate the manna in the wilderness, and they died. This is the bread which comes down from heaven, that a man may eat of it and not die. I am the living bread which comes down from heaven; if any one eats of this bread, he will live for ever, and the bread which I shall give for the life of the world is my flesh.'

The Jews then disputed among themselves, saying, 'How can this man give us his flesh to eat?' So Jesus said to them, 'Truly, truly, I say to you, unless you eat the flesh of the Son of man and drink his blood, you have no life in you; he who eats my flesh and drinks my blood has eternal life, and I will raise him up at the last day. For my flesh is food indeed, and my blood is drink indeed. He who eats my flesh and drinks my blood abides in me, and I in him. As the living Father sent me, and I live because of the Father, so he who eats me will live because of me. This is the bread which came down from heaven, not such as the fathers ate and died; he who eats this bread will live for ever.' This he said in the synagogue, as he taught at Capernaum.

Jn 6:68,69 Simon Peter answered him, 'Lord, to whom shall we go? You have the words of eternal life; and we have believed, and have come to know, you are the Holy One of God.'

Jn 5:21 'For as the Father raises the dead and gives them life, so also the Son gives life to whom he will.'

Jn 5:24-29 'Truly, truly, I say to you, he who hears my word and believes him who sent me, has eternal life; he does not come into judgment, but has passed from death to life.

'Truly, truly, I say to you, the hour is coming, and now is, when the dead will hear the voice of the Son of God, and those who hear will live. For as the Father has life in himself, so he has granted the Son also to have life in himself, and he has given him authority to execute judgment, because he is the Son of man. Do not marvel at this; for the hour is coming when all who are in the tombs will hear his voice and come forth, those who have done good, to the resurrection of life, and those who have done evil, to the resurrection of judgment.'

Jn 5:39,40 'You search the scriptures, because you think that in them you have eternal life; and it is they that bear witness to me; yet you refuse to come to me that you may have life.'

Jn 10:10 'The thief comes only to steal and kill and destroy; I come that you may have life, and have it abundantly.'

Jn 10:28 '. . . and I give them eternal life, and they shall never perish, and no one shall snatch them out of my hand.'

Jn 11:25,26 Martha said to him, 'I know that he will rise again in the resurrection at the last day.' Jesus said to her, 'I am the resurrection and the life; he who believes in me, though he die, yet shall he live . . . .'

Jn 12:23-25 And Jesus answered them, 'The hour has come for the Son of man to be glorified. Truly, truly, I say to you, unless a grain of wheat falls into the earth and dies, it remains alone; but if it dies, it bears much fruit. He who loves his life loses it, and he who hates his life in this world will keep it for eternal life.'

Jn 17:3 — 'And this is eternal life, that they know thee the only true God and Jesus Christ whom thou hast sent.'

Mt. 26:26-28 — Now as they were eating, Jesus took bread, and blessed and broke it, gave it to the disciples and said, 'Take, eat; this is my body.' And he took a cup, and when he had given thanks he gave it to them, saying, 'Drink of it, all of you; for this is my blood of the covenant, which is poured out for many for the forgiveness of sins.'

ii. Jesus as Bridegroom

Jn 3:29,30 — 'He who has the bride is the bridegroom; the friend of the bridegroom, who stands and hears him, rejoices greatly at the bridegroom's voice; therefore this joy of mine is now full. He must increase, but I must decrease.'

Mt. 9:15 — And Jesus said to them, 'Can the wedding guests mourn as long as the bridegroom is with them? The days will come, when the bridegroom is taken away from them, and then they will fast.'

Lk. 12:35,36 — 'Let your loins be girded and your lamps burning, and be like men who are waiting for their master to come home from the wedding feast, so that they may open to him at once when he comes and knocks.'

Mt. 22:2 — 'The kingdom of God may be compared to a king who gave a marriage feast for his son . . . .'

Mt. 25:1 — 'Then the kingdom of heaven shall be compared to ten maidens who took their lamps and went to meet the bridegroom.'

Mt. 25:10 — 'And while they went to buy, the bridegroom came, and those who were ready went in with him to the marriage feast; and the door was shut.'

iii. Jesus and Water

Mt. 3:13-17 — Then Jesus came from Galilee to the Jordan to John, to be baptized by him. John would have prevented him, saying, 'I need to be baptized by you, and do you come to me?' But Jesus answered him, 'Let it be so now; for thus it is fitting for us to fulfil all righteousness.' Then he consented. And when Jesus was baptized, he went up immediately from the water, and behold, the heavens were opened and he saw the Spirit of God descending like a dove, and alighting on him; and lo, a voice from heaven, saying, 'This is my beloved Son, with whom I am well pleased.'

Jn 1:33 — 'I myself did not know him; but he who sent me to baptize with water said to me, "He on whom you see the Spirit descend and remain, this is he who baptizes with the Holy Spirit." '

Jn 2:1-11 — On the third day there was a marriage at Cana in Galilee, and the mother of Jesus was there; Jesus also was invited to the marriage, with his disciples. When the wine failed, the mother of Jesus said to him, 'They have no wine.' And Jesus said to her, 'O woman, what have you to do with me? My hour has not yet come.' His mother said to the servants, 'Do whatever he tells you.' Now six stone jars were standing there, for the Jewish rites of purification, each holding twenty or thirty gallons. Jesus said to them, 'Fill the jars with water.' And they filled them up to the brim. He said to them, 'Now draw some out, and take it to the steward of the feast.' So they took it. When the steward of the feast tasted the water now become wine, he did not know where it had come from (though the servants who had drawn the water knew), the steward of the feast called the bridegroom and said to him, 'Every man serves the good wine first; and when men have drunk freely, then the poor wine; but you have kept the good wine until now.' This, the first of his signs, Jesus did at Cana in Galilee, and manifested his glory; and his disciples believed in him.

Jn 3:22 — After this Jesus and his disciples went into the land of Judea; there he remained with them and baptized.

Jn 2:25,26 — Now a discussion arose between John's disciples and a Jew over purifying. And they came to John, and said to him, 'Rabbi, he who was with you beyond the Jordan, to whom you bore witness, here he is, baptizing, and all are going to him.'

Jn 4:7,15 — There came a woman of Samaria to draw water. Jesus said to her, 'Give me a drink.' For his disciples had gone away into the city to buy food. The Samaritan woman said to him, 'How is it that you, a Jew, ask a drink of me, a woman of Samaria?' For Jews have no dealings with Samaritans. Jesus answered her, 'If you knew the gift of God, and who it is that is saying to you, "Give me a drink," you would have asked him and he would have given you living water.' The woman said to him, 'Sir, you have nothing to draw with, and the well is deep; where do you get that living water? Are you greater than our father Jacob, who gave us the well, and drank from it himself, and his sons and his cattle?' Jesus said to her, 'Every one who drinks of this water will thirst again, but whoever drinks of the water that I shall give him will never thirst; the water that I shall give him will become in him a spring of water welling up to eternal life.' The woman said to him, 'Sir, give me this water, that I may not thirst, nor come here to draw.'

Jn 6:35 Jesus said to them, 'I am the bread of life; he who comes to me shall not hunger, and he who believes in me shall never thirst.'

Jn 7:37-39 On the last day of the feast, the great day, Jesus stood up and proclaimed, 'If any one thirst, let him come to me and drink. He who believes in me, as the scripture has said, "Out of his heart shall flow rivers of living water." Now this he said about the Spirit, which those who believed in him were to receive; for as yet the Spirit had not been given, because Jesus was not yet glorified.

Jn 19:34-37 But one of the soldiers pierced his side with a spear, and at once there came out blood and water. He who saw it has borne witness – his testimony is true, and he knows that he tells the truth – that you also may believe. For these things took place that the scripture might be fulfilled. 'Not a bone of him shall be broken.' And again another scripture says, 'They shall look on him whom they have pierced.'

iv. Jesus and Light

Jn 1:4-7 In him was life, and the life was the light of men. The light shines in the darkness, and the darkness cannot overcome it. There was a man sent from God, whose name was John. He came for testimony, to bear witness to the light, that all might believe through him.

Lk. 2:32 '. . . a light for revelation to the Gentiles, and for the glory of thy people Israel.'

Jn 3:19-21 And this is the judgment, that the light has come into the world, and men loved darkness rather than light because their deeds were evil. For every one who does evil hates the light, and does not come to the light, lest his deeds should be exposed. But he who does what is true comes to the light that it may be clearly seen that his deeds have been wrought in God.

Mt. 4:16 '. . . the people who sat in darkness
have seen a great light,
and for those who sat in the region and shadow of death
light has dawned.'

Jn 8:12 And again Jesus spoke to them, saying, 'I am the light of the world; he who follows me will not walk in darkness, but will have the light of life.'

Jn 9:5 'As long as I am in the world, I am the light of the world.'

Mt. 5:14-16 'You are the light of the world. A city set on a hill cannot be hid. Nor do men light a lamp and put it under a bushel, but on a stand, and it gives light to all in the house. Let your light so shine before men, that they may see your good works and give glory to your Father who is in heaven.'

Jn 12:35,36 Jesus said to them, 'The light is with you for a little longer. Walk while you have the light, lest the darkness overtake you; he who walks in the darkness does not know where he goes. While you have the light, believe in the light, that you may become sons of light.'

Jn 12:46 'I have come as light into the world, that whoever believes in me may not remain in darkness.'

8. Jesus: God Speaks of Him

i. Jesus speaks of himself

Lk. 2:49	And he said to them, 'How is it that you sought me? Did you not know that I must be in my Father's house?'
Jn 1:51	(said to Nathanael) And he said to him, 'Truly, truly, I say to you, you will see heaven opened, and the angels of God ascending and descending upon the Son of man.'
Jn 2:19	Jesus answered them, 'Destroy this temple, and in three days I will raise it up.'
Jn 3:14	'. . . and as Moses lifted up the serpent in the wilderness, so must the Son of man be lifted up . . . .'
Jn 4:34	Jesus said to them, 'My food is to do the will of him who sent me, and to accomplish his work.'
Jn 4:44	For Jesus himself testified that a prophet has no honour in his own country.
Lk. 4:21	And he began to say to them, 'Today this scripture has been fulfilled in your hearing.'
Mt. 12:6	'. . . I tell you, something greater than the temple is here.'
Lk. 7:22,23	And he answered them, 'Go and tell John what you have seen and heard; the blind receive their sight, the lame walk, lepers are cleansed, and the deaf hear, the dead are raised up, the poor have good news preached to them. And blessed is he who takes no offence at me.'
Mk 6:4	And Jesus said to them, 'A prophet is not without honour, except in his own country, and among his own kin, and in his own house.'
Mt. 14:27	But immediately he spoke to them, saying, 'Take heart, it is I; have no fear.'
Jn 6:32	Jesus said to them, 'Truly, truly, I say to you, it was not Moses who gave you the bread from heaven; my Father gives you the true bread from heaven.'
Jn 6:35	Jesus said to them, 'I am the bread of life; he who comes to me shall not hunger, and he who believes in me shall never thirst.'

Jn 6:46	'... Not that anyone has seen the Father except him who is from God; he has seen the Father.'
Jn 6:51,52	'... I am the living bread which came down from heaven; if anyone eats of this bread, he will live for ever; and the bread which I shall give for the life of the world is my flesh.' The Jews then disputed among themselves, saying, 'How can this man give us his flesh to eat?'
Jn 6:54	'... he who eats my flesh and drinks my blood has eternal life, and I will raise him up at the last day.'
Jn 5:17	But Jesus answered them, 'My Father is working still, and I am working.'
Jn 5:22	'... The Father judges no one, but has given all judgment to the Son ....'
Jn 5:26	'... For as the Father has life in himself, so he has granted the Son also to have life in himself ....'
Jn 5:30	'I can do nothing on my own authority; as I hear, I judge; and my judgment is just, because I seek not my own will but the will of him who sent me.'
Jn 5:36,37	'... But the testimony which I have is greater than that of John; for the works which the Father has granted me to accomplish, these very works which I am doing, bear me witness that the Father has sent me. And the Father who sent me has himself borne witness to me. His voice you have never heard, his form you have never seen ....'
Jn 5:43	'... I have come in my Father's name, and you do not receive me; if another comes in his own name, him you will receive.'
Jn 7:28	So Jesus proclaimed, as he taught in the temple, 'You know me, and you know where I am come from? But I have not come of my own accord; he who sent me is true, and him you do not know.'
Jn 8:12	Again, Jesus spoke to them, saying, 'I am the light of the world; he who follows me will not walk in darkness, but will have the light of life.'
Jn 8:25	They said to him, 'Who are you?' Jesus said to them, 'Even what I have told you from the beginning.'

Jn 8:42	Jesus said to them, 'If God were your Father, you would love me, for I proceeded and came forth from God; I came not of my own accord, but he sent me.'
Jn 8:58	Jesus said to them, 'Truly, truly, I say to you, before Abraham was, I am.'
Jn 9:5	'... As long as I am in the world, I am the light of the world.'
Jn 9:35	Jesus heard that they had cast him out, and having found him he said, 'Do you believe in the Son of man?'
Jn 10:7-11	So Jesus again said to them, 'Truly, truly, I say to you, I am the door of the sheep. All who come before me are thieves and robbers; but the sheep did not heed them. I am the door; if anyone enters by me he will be saved and will go in and out and find pasture. The thief comes purely to steal and kill and destroy; I came that they may have life, and have it abundantly, I am the good shepherd. The good shepherd lays down his life for the sheep.'
Jn 10:14	'... I am the good shepherd; I know my own and my own know me.'
Mt. 11:27	'... All things have been delivered to me by my Father; and no one knows the Son except the Father, and no one knows the Father except the Son and any one to whom the Son chooses to reveal him.'
Mt. 12:41,42	'... The men of Nineveh will arise at the judgment with this generation and condemn it; for they repented at the preaching of Jonah, and behold, something greater than Jonah is here. The queen of the South will arise at the judgment with this generation and condemn it; for she came from the ends of the earth to hear the wisdom of Solomon, and behold something greater than Solomon is here.'
Lk. 12:13,14	One of the multitude said to him, 'Teacher, bid my brother divide the inheritance with me.' But he said to him, 'Man, who made me a judge or divider over you?'
Jn 10:24,25	So the Jews gathered round him and said to him, 'How long will you keep us in suspense? If you are the Christ, tell us plainly.' Jesus answered them, 'I told you, and you

do not believe. The works that I do in my Father's name, they bear witness to me . . . .'

Jn 10:30	'. . . I and the Father are one.'
Lk. 18:19	And Jesus said to him, 'Why do you call me good? No one is good but God alone.'
Jn 11:25	Jesus said to her, 'I am the resurrection and the life; he who believes in me, though he die, yet shall he live . . . .'
Jn 11:41,42	So they took away the stone. And Jesus lifted up his eyes and said, 'Father, I thank thee that thou hast heard me. I knew that thou hearest me always, but I have said this on account of the people standing by, that they may believe that thou didst send me.'
Mt. 20:28	'. . . even as the Son of man came not to be served but to serve, and to give his life as a ransom for many.'
Mk 14:6-8	(said of Mary Magdalene) But Jesus said, 'Let her alone; why do you trouble her? She has done a beautiful thing to me. For you always have the poor with you, and whenever you will, you can do good to them; but you will not always have me. She has done what she could; she has anointed my body beforehand for burying.'
Jn 12:26	'If anyone serves me, he must follow me; and where I am, there shall my servant be also; if any one serves me, the Father will honour him.'
Jn 12:32	'. . . and I, when I am lifted up from the earth, will draw all men to myself.'
Mt. 25:37-40	. . . Then the righteous will answer him, 'Lord, when did we see thee hungry and feed thee, or thirsty and give thee drink? And when did we see thee a stranger and welcome thee, or naked and cloth thee? and when did we see thee sick or in prison and visit thee?' And the King will answer them, 'Truly I say to you, as you did it to one of the least of these my brethren, you did it to me.'
Lk. 22:27	'. . . For which is the greater, one who sits at table, or one who serves? Is it not the one who sits at table? But I am among you as one who serves.'

Jn 13:13 'You call me Teacher and Lord; and you are right, for so I am.'

Mt. 26:31 Then Jesus said to them, 'You will all fall away because of me this night; for it is written, "I will strike the shepherd, and the sheep of the flock will be scattered." '

Jn 14:6-10 Jesus said to him, 'I am the way, and the truth, and the life; no one comes to the Father but by me. If you had known me, you would have known my Father also; henceforth you know him and have seen him.'

Philip said to him, 'Lord, show us the Father, and we shall be satisfied.' Jesus said to him, 'Have I been with you so long, and yet you do not know me, Philip? He who has seen me has seen the Father, how can you say, "Show us the Father"'? Do you not believe that I am in the Father and the Father in me? The words that I say to you I do not speak on my own authority; but the Father who dwells in me does his works.'

Jn 15:1 'I am the true vine, and my Father is the vinedresser.'

Jn 15:5 '. . . I am the vine, you are the branches. He who abides in me, and I in him, he it is that bears much fruit, for apart from me you can do nothing.'

Jn 16:25-28 'I have said this to you in figures; the hour is coming when I shall no longer speak to you in figures but tell you plainly of the Father. In that day you will ask in my name; and I do not say to you that I shall pray the Father for you; for the Father himself loves you, because you have loved me and have believed that I came from the Father. I came from the Father and have come into the world; again, I am leaving the world and going to the Father.'

Jn 16:32 '. . . The hour is coming, indeed it has come, when you will be scattered, every man to his home, and will leave me alone; yet I am not alone, for the Father is with me.'

Jn 17:3 '. . . And this is eternal life, that they know thee the only true God, and Jesus Christ whom thou hast sent.'

Mt. 26:63,64 But Jesus was silent. And the high priest said to him, 'I adjure you by the living God, tell us if you are the Christ, the Son of God.' Jesus said to him, 'You have said so. But I tell you, hereafter you will see the Son of man seated at the right hand of Power, and coming on the clouds of heaven.'

Jn 18:37 Pilate said to him, 'So you are a king?' Jesus answered, 'You say that I am a king. For this I was born, and for this I have come into the world, to bear witness to the truth. Everyone who is of the truth hears my voice.'

Lk. 24:38-40 And he said to them, 'Why are you troubled, and why do questionings rise in your hearts? See my hands and my feet, that it is I myself; handle me, and see; for a spirit has not flesh and bones as you see that I have.' And when he had said this, he showed them his hands and his feet.

Mt. 28:18-20 And Jesus came and said to them, 'All authority in heaven and on earth has been given to me. Go therefore and make disciples of all nations, baptizing them in the name of the Father and of the Son and of the Holy Spirit, teaching them to observe all that I have commanded you; and lo, I am with you always, to the close of the age.'

ii. 'I am' passages

Jn 17:3 'I am.'

Jn 6:35 'I am the bread of life.'

Jn 6:48 'I am the bread of life.'

Jn 6:51 'I am the living bread.'

Jn 9:5 'I am the light of the world.'

Jn 10:7,9 'I am the door of the sheep-fold.'

Jn 10:11,14 'I am the Good Shepherd.'

Jn 11.25	'I am the resurrection and the life.'
Jn 14:6	'I am the way and the truth and the life.'
Jn 15:5	'I am the vine.'

iii. The Father speaks of Jesus

Mk 1:11	. . . and a voice came from heaven, 'Thou are my beloved Son; with thee I am well pleased.'
Jn 1:33	(Spoken by John the Baptist) '. . . I myself did not know him; but he who sent me to baptize with water said to me, "He on whom you see the Spirit descend and remain, this is he who baptizes with the Holy Spirit." '
Mt. 17:5	He was still speaking, when lo, a bright cloud overshadowed them, and a voice from the cloud said, 'This is my beloved Son, with whom I am well pleased; listen to him.'
Jn 12:28	Then a voice came from heaven, 'I have glorified it, and I will glorify it again.'

iv. Scripture speaks of Jesus

Mt. 2:6	'And you, O Bethlehem, in the land of Judah, are by no means least among the rulers of Judah; for from you shall come a ruler who will govern my people Israel.'
Mt. 2:15	This was to fulfil what the Lord had spoken by the prophet, 'Out of Egypt have I called my son.'
Lk. 3:6	'. . . And all flesh shall see the salvation of God.'
Lk. 4:18,19	'The Spirit of the Lord is upon me, because he has anointed me to preach good news to the poor. He has sent me to proclaim release to the captives, and recovering of sight to the blind, to set at liberty those who are oppressed, to proclaim the acceptable year of the Lord.'
Mt. 4:16	'. . . The people who sat in darkness have seen a great light, and for those who sat in the region and shadow of death light has dawned.'

Mt. 8:17 — This was to fulfil what was spoken by the prophet Isaiah, 'He took our infirmities and bore our diseases.'

Mt. 12:18-21 — 'Behold my servant whom I have chosen, my beloved with whom my soul is well pleased. I will put my Spirit upon him, and he shall proclaim justice to the Gentiles. He will not wrangle or cry aloud, nor will anyone hear his voice in the streets; he will not break a bruised reed or quench a smouldering wick, till he brings justice to victory; and in his name will the Gentiles hope.'

Mt. 22:43-44 — 'How is it then that David, inspired by the Spirit, calls him Lord, saying,

"The Lord said to my Lord,
Sit at my right hand,
till I put the enemies under thy feet"?'

Mt. 21:5 — 'Tell the daughter of Zion, Behold your king is coming to you, humble and mounted on an ass, and on a colt, the foal of an ass.'

Mt. 27:46 — And about the ninth hour Jesus cried with a loud voice, 'Eli, Eli, lama sabach-thani?' that is, 'My God, my God, why has thou forsaken me?'

Jn 19:36,37 — For these things took place that the scripture might be fulfilled, 'Not a bone of him shall be broken.' And again another scripture says, 'They shall look on him whom they have pierced.'

Lk. 24:27 — And beginning with Moses and all the prophets, he interpreted to them in all the scriptures the things concerning himself.

Lk. 24:44,45 — Then he said to them, 'These are my words which I spoke to you, while I was still with you, that everything written about me in the law of Moses and the prophets and the psalms must be fulfilled.' Then he opened their minds to understand the scriptures.

9. Jesus: Attitudes to Him

i. The attitude of those who loved him

Jn 1:15-18 (John bore witness to him, and cried, 'This was he of whom I said, "He who comes after me ranks before me, for he was before me."') And from his fulness have we all received, grace upon grace. For the law was given through Moses; grace and truth came through Jesus Christ. No one has ever seen God; the only Son, who is in the bosom of the Father, he has made him known.

Lk. 1:31-33 '. . . and behold, you will conceive in your womb and bear a son, and you shall call his name Jesus. He will be great, and will be called the Son of the Most High; and the Lord God will give to him the throne of his father David, and he will reign over the house of Jacob for ever . . . .'

Lk. 1:43 '. . . Any why is this granted me, that the mother of my Lord should come to me?'

Lk. 1:69 '. . . and has raised up a horn of salvation for us.

Lk. 1:76 '. . . and you, child, will be called the prophet of the Most High . . . .'

Mt. 1:20,21 But as he considered this, behold, an angel of the Lord appeared to him in a dream, saying, 'Joseph, son of David, do not fear to take Mary your wife, for that which is conceived in her is of the Holy Spirit; she will bear a son, and you shall call his name Jesus, for he will save his people from their sins.'

Lk. 2:11,12 '. . . For to you is born this day in the city of David a Saviour, who is Christ the Lord. And this will be a sign for you: you will find a babe wrapped in swaddling cloths and lying in a manger.'

Lk. 2:29-32 'Lord, now lettest thou thy servant depart in peace, according to thy word; for mine eyes have seen thy salvation which thou hast prepared in the presence of all peoples, a light for revelation to the Gentiles, and for glory to thy people Israel.'

Lk. 2:34 ... and Simeon blessed them and said to Mary his mother, 'Behold, this child is set for the fall and rising of many in Israel, and for a sign that is spoken against ....'

Mt. 2:2 'Where is he who has been born king of the Jews? For we have seen his star in the East, and have come to worship him.'

Lk. 3:16,17 John answered them all, 'I baptize you with water; but he who is mightier than I is coming, the thong of whose sandals I am not worthy to untie; he will baptize you with the Holy Spirit and with fire. His winnowing fork is in his hand, to clear his threshing floor, and to gather the wheat into his granary, but the chaff he will burn with unquenchable fire.'

Mt. 3:14 John would have prevented him, saying, 'I need to be baptized by you, and do you come to me?'

Jn 1:26-36 John answered them, 'I baptize with water; but among you stands one whom you do not know, even he who comes after me, the thong of whose sandal I am not worthy to untie.' This took place in Bethany beyond the Jordan, where John was baptizing.

The next day he saw Jesus coming toward him, and said, 'Behold, the Lamb of God, who takes away the sin of the world! This is he of whom I said, "After me comes a man who ranks before me, for he was before me." I myself did not know him; but for this I came baptizing with water, that he might be revealed to Israel.' And John bore witness, 'I saw the Spirit descend as a dove from heaven, and it remained on him. I myself did not know him; but he who sent me to baptize with water said to me, "He on whom you see the Spirit descend and remain, this is he who baptizes with the Holy Spirit." And I have seen and have borne witness that this is the Son of God.'

The next day again John was standing with two of his disciples; and he looked at Jesus as he walked, and said, 'Behold, the Lamb of God.'

Jn 1:45 Philip found Nathanael, and said to him, 'We have found him of whom Moses in the law and also the prophets wrote, Jesus of Nazareth, the Son of Joseph.'

Jn 1:49 — Nathanael answered him, 'Rabbi, you are the Son of God. You are the King of Israel.'

Jn 2:5 — His mother said to the servants, 'Do whatever he tells you.'

Jn 3:29-31 — 'He who has the bride is the bridegroom: the friend of the bridegroom, who stands and hears him, rejoices greatly at the bridegroom's voice; therefore this joy of mine is now full. He must increase, but I must decrease.'

He who comes from above is above all: he who is of the earth belongs to the earth, and of the earth he speaks; he who comes from heaven is above all.

Jn 4:29 — 'Come, see a man who told me all that I ever did. Can this be the Christ?' They went out of the city and were coming to him.

Jn 4:42 — They said to the woman, 'It is no longer because of your words that we believe, for we have heard for ourselves, and we know that this is indeed the Saviour of the world.'

Lk. 4:22 — And all spoke well of him, and wondered at the gracious words which proceeded out of his mouth; and they said, 'Is not this Joseph's son?'

Mt. 7:28 — And when Jesus finished these sayings, the crowds were astonished at his teaching, for he taught them as one who had authority, and not as their scribes.

Mk 1:28 — And at once his fame spread everywhere throughout all the surrounding region of Galilee.

Mk 1:37 — . . . and they found him and said to him, 'Everyone is searching for you.'

Lk. 5:8 — But when Simon Peter saw it, he fell down at Jesus' knees, saying, 'Depart from me, for I am a sinful man, O Lord.'

Lk. 5:26 — And amazement seized them all, and they glorified God and were filled with awe, saying, 'We have seen strange things today.

Mt. 4:24 — So his fame spread throughout all Syria, and they brought him all the sick, those afflicted with various diseases and pains, demoniacs, epileptics, and paralytics, and he healed them.

Mt. 8:8,9	But the centurion answered him, 'Lord, I am not worthy to have you come under my roof; but only say the word, and my servant will be healed. For I am a man under authority, with soldiers under me; and I say to one, "Go" and he goes, and to another "Come", and he comes, and to my slave "Do this", and he does it.'
Lk. 7:19	And John, calling to him two of his disciples, sent them to the Lord, saying, 'Are you he who is to come, or shall we look for another?'
Lk. 7:44-47	Then turning toward the woman he said to Simon, 'Do you see this woman? I entered your house, you gave me no water for my feet, but she has wet my feet with her tears and wiped them with her hair. You gave me no kiss, but from the time I came in she has not ceased to kiss my feet. You did not anoint my head with oil, but she has anointed my feet with ointment. Therefore I tell you, her sins, which are many, are forgiven, for she loved much; but he who is forgiven little, loves little.'
Mk 3:20,21	. . . and the crowd came together again, so that they could not even eat. And when his friends heard it, they went out to seize him, for they said, 'He is beside himself.'
Mk 4:41	And they were filled with awe, and said to one another, 'Who then is this, that even wind and sea obey him?'
Mt. 9:20,21	And behold, a woman who had suffered from a hemorrhage for twelve years came up behind him and touched the fringe of his garment; for she said to herself, 'If I only touch his garment, I shall be made well.'
Mt. 14:26	But when the disciples saw him walking on the sea, they were terrified, saying, 'It is a ghost.' And they cried out for fear.
Mt. 14:33	And those in the boat worshipped him, saying, 'Truly, you are the Son of God.'
Jn 6:69	'. . . and we have believed, and have come to know, that you are the Holy One of God.'
Mt. 16:15,16	He said to them, 'But who do you say that I am?' Simon Peter replied, 'You are the Christ, the Son of the living God.'

Jn 9:30-33 The man answered, 'Why, this is a marvel. You do not know where he comes from, and yet he opened my eyes. We know that God does not listen to sinners, but if any one is a worshipper of God and does his will, God listens to him. Never since the world began has it been heard that any one opened the eyes of a man born blind. If this man were not from God, he could do nothing.'

Lk. 10:40 But Martha was distracted with much serving; and she went to him and said, 'Lord, do you not care that my sister has left me to serve alone? Tell her then to help me.'

Mt. 9:28 When he entered the house, the blind men came to him; and Jesus said to them, 'Do you believe that I am able to do this?' They said to him, 'Yes, Lord.'

Mt. 9:31 But they went away and spread his fame through all that district.

Lk. 11:27 As he said this, a woman in the crowd raised her voice and said to him, 'Blessed is the womb that bore you, and the breasts that you sucked.'

Jn 11:21 Martha said to Jesus, 'Lord, if you had been here, my brother would not have died.'

Jn 11:27 She said to him, 'Yes, Lord; I believe that you are the Christ, the Son of God, who is coming into the world.'

Jn 11:32 Then Mary, when she came where Jesus was and saw him, fell at his feet, saying to him, 'Lord, if you had been here, my brother would not have died.'

Mt. 21:9,10 And the crowds that went before him and that followed him shouted, 'Hosanna to the son of David! Blessed is he that comes in the name of the Lord! Hosanna in the highest!' And when he entered Jerusalem, all the city was stirred, saying, 'Who is this?' And the crowds said, 'This is the prophet Jesus from Nazareth of Galilee.'

Jn 16:29,30 His disciples said, 'Ah, now you are speaking plainly, not in any figure. Now we know that you know all things, and need none to question you; by this we believe that you came from God.'

Mk 14:50 And they all forsook him, and fled.

Mt. 26:58	But Peter followed him at a distance, as far as the courtyard of the high priest, and going inside he sat with the guards to see the end.
Mt. 26:72-74	And again he denied it with an oath, 'I do not know the man.' After a little while the bystanders came up and said to Peter, 'Certainly you are also one of them, for your accent betrays you.' Then he began to invoke a curse on himself and to swear, 'I do not know the man.' And immediately the cock crowed.
Lk. 23:41,42	'. . . And we indeed justly; for we are receiving the due reward of our deeds; but this man has done nothing wrong.' And he said to him, 'Jesus, remember me when you come in your kingly power.'
Mt. 28:5,6	But the angel said to the woman, 'Do not be afraid; for I know that you seek Jesus who was crucified. He is not here; for he has risen, as he said. Come, see the place where he lay.'
Jn 20:15	Jesus said to her, 'Woman, why are you weeping? Whom do you seek?' Supposing him to be the gardener, she said to him, 'Sir, if you have carried him away, tell me where you have laid him, and I will take him away.'
Lk. 24:32	They said to each other, 'Did not our hearts burn within us while he talked to us on the road, while he opened to us the scriptures?'
Jn 20:20	When he had said this, he showed them his hands and his side. Then the disciples were glad when they saw the Lord.
Jn 20:28	Thomas answered him, 'My Lord and my God.'
Jn 20:31	. . . but these are written that you may believe that Jesus is the Christ, the Son of God, and that believing you may have life in his name.

ii. The attitude of the uncommitted

Jn 1:46	Nathanael said to him, 'Can anything good come out of Nazareth?' Philip said to him, 'Come and see.'
Jn 3:26	And they came to John, and said to him, 'Rabbi, he who was with you beyond the Jordan, to whom you bore

witness, here he is, baptizing, and all are going to him.'

Jn 4:9 The Samaritan woman said to him, 'How is it that you, a Jew, ask a drink of me, a woman of Samaria?' For Jews have no dealings with Samaritans.

Jn 4:19 The woman said to him, 'Sir, I perceive that you are a prophet.'

Mk 1:45 But he went out and began to talk freely about it, and to spread the news, so that Jesus could no longer openly enter a town, but was out in the country; and people came to him from every quarter.

Lk. 8:37 Then all the people of the surrounding country of the Gerasenes asked him to depart from them; for they were seized with great fear; so he got into the boat and returned.

Mt. 9:24-26 . . . he said, 'Depart; for the girl is not dead but sleeping.' And they laughed at him. But when the crowd had been put outside, he went in and took her by the hand, and the girl arose. And the report of this went through all that district.

Mk 6:2,3 And on the sabbath he began to teach in the synagogue; and many who heard him were astonished, saying, 'Where did this man get all this? What is the wisdom given to him? What mighty works are wrought by his hands! Is not this the carpenter, the son of Mary and brother of James and Joses and Judas and Simon, and are not his sisters here with us?' And they took offence at him.

Jn 6:42 They said, 'Is not this Jesus, the son of Joseph, whose father and mother we know? How does he now say, "I have come down from heaven"?'

Mt. 15:31 . . . so that the throng wondered when they saw the dumb speaking, the maimed whole, the lame walking, and the blind seeing; and they glorified the God of Israel.

Mt. 16:13,14 Now when Jesus came into the district of Caesarea Philippi, he asked his disciples, 'Who do men say that the Son of man is?' And they said, 'Some say John the Baptist, others say Elijah, and others Jeremiah or one of the prophets.'

Mk 9:14	And when they came to the disciples, they saw a great crowd about them, and scribes arguing with them.
Jn 7:5	For even his brethren did not believe in him.
Jn 7:12	And there was much muttering about him among the people. While some said, 'He is a good man,' others said, 'No, he is leading the people astray.'
Jn 7:25-28	Some of the people of Jerusalem therefore said, 'Is not this the man whom they seek to kill? And here he is, speaking openly, and they say nothing to him. Can it be that the authorities really know that this is the Christ? Yet we know where this man comes from; and when the Christ appears, no one will know where he comes from.' So Jesus proclaimed, as he taught in the temple, 'You know me, and you know where I come from? But I have not come of my own accord; he who sent me is true, and him you do not know.'
Jn 7:31	Yet many of the people believed in him; they said, 'When the Christ appears, will he do more signs than this man has done?'
Jn 7:40,41	When they heard these words, some of the people said, 'This is really the prophet.' Others said, 'This is the Christ.' But some said, 'Is the Christ to come from Galilee?'
Jn 7:46	The officers answered, 'No man ever spoke like this man.'
Jn 9:16	Some of the Pharisees said, 'This man is not from God, for he does not keep the sabbath.' But others said, 'How can a man who is a sinner do such signs?' There was a division among them.
Jn 9:25	He answered, 'Whether he is a sinner, I do not know; one thing I know, that though I was blind, now I see.'
Jn 10:21	Others said, 'These are not the saying of one who has a demon. Can a demon open the eyes of the blind?'
Mt. 12:23	And all the people were amazed, and said, 'Can this be the Son of David?'
Lk. 11:38	The Pharisee was astonished to see that he did not first wash before dinner.

Mk 14:4,5 But there were some who said to themselves indignantly, 'Why was the ointment thus wasted? For this ointment might have been sold for more than three hundred denarii, and given to the poor.' And they reproached her.

Jn 12:37,38 Though he had done so many signs before them, yet they did not believe in him; it was that the word spoken by the prophet Isaiah might be fulfilled:
'Lord, who has believed our report,
and to whom has the arm of the Lord been revealed?'

Mt. 21:10,11 And when he entered Jerusalem, all the city was stirred, saying, 'Who is this?' And the crowds said, 'This is the prophet Jesus from Nazareth of Galilee.'

Lk. 19:47,48 And he was teaching daily in the temple. The chief priests and the scribes and the principal men of the people sought to destroy him; but they did not find anything they could do, for all the people hung upon his words.

Mt. 21:46 But when they tried to arrest him, they feared the multitudes, because they held him to be a prophet.

Jn 18:33 Pilate entered the praetorium again and called Jesus, and said to him, 'Are you the King of the Jews?'

Lk. 23:14-16 'You brought me this man as one who was perverting the people; and after examining him before you, behold, I did not find this man guilty of any of your charges against him; neither did Herod, for he sent him back to us. Behold, nothing deserving death has been done by him; I will therefore chastise him and release him.'

Lk. 23:22 A third time he said to them, 'Why, what evil has he done? I have found in him no crime deserving death; I will therefore chastise him and release him.'

Mt. 27:19 Besides, while he was sitting on the judgment seat, his wife sent word to him, 'Have nothing to do with that righteous man, for I have suffered much over him today in a dream.'

Jn 19:4 Pilate went out again, and said to them, 'Behold, I am bringing him out to you, that you may know that I find no crime in him.'

Jn 19:19	Pilate also wrote a title and put it on the cross; it read, 'Jesus of Nazareth, the King of the Jews.'
Mk 15:39	And when the centurion, who stood facing him, saw that he thus breathed his last, he said, 'Truly this man was the Son of God.'
Lk. 24:19	And he said to them, 'What things?' And they said to him, 'Concerning Jesus of Nazareth, who was a prophet mighty in deed and word before God and all the people . . . .'

iii The attitude of his enemies

Mk 1:24	. . . and he cried out, 'What have you to do with us, Jesus of Nazareth? Have you come to destroy us? I know who you are, the Holy One of God.'
Lk. 4:41	And demons also came out of many crying, 'You are the Son of God.' But he rebuked them, and would not allow them to speak, because they knew that he was the Christ.
Lk. 5:21	And the scribes and the Pharisees began to question, saying, 'Who is this that speaks blasphemies? Who can forgive sins but God only?'
Mt. 9:11	And when the Pharisees saw this, they said to his disciples, 'Why does your teacher eat with tax collectors and sinners?'
Lk. 7:34	The Son of man has come eating and drinking; and you say, 'Behold, a glutton and a drunkard, a friend of tax collectors and sinners.'
Lk. 7:39	Now when the Pharisees who had invited him saw it, he said to himself, 'If this man were a prophet, he would have known who and what sort of woman this is who is touching him, for she is a sinner.'
Mt. 8:29	And behold, they cried out, 'What have you to do with us, O Son of God? Have you come here to torment us before the time?'
Mk 6:14-16	King Herod heard of it; for Jesus' name had become known. Some said, 'John the baptizer has been raised from the dead; that is why these powers are at work in him.' But others said, 'It is Elijah.' And others said, 'It is a prophet, like one of the prophets of old.' But when

	Herod heard of it, he said, 'John, whom I beheaded, has been raised.'
Mt. 15:12	Then the disciples came and said to him, 'Do you know that the Pharisees were offended when they heard this saying?'
Jn 7:52	They replied, 'Are you from Galilee too? Search and you will see that no prophet is to rise from Galilee.'
Jn 8:13	The Pharisees then said to him, 'You are bearing witness to yourself; your testimony is not true.'
Jn 8:48	The Jews answered him, 'Are we not right in saying that you are a Samaritan and have a demon?'
Jn 8:53	'Are you greater than our father Abraham, who died? And the prophets died! Who do you claim to be?'
Jn 9:16	Some of the Pharisees said, 'This man is not from God, for he does not keep the Sabbath.' But others said, 'How can a man who is a sinner do such signs?' There was a division among them.
Jn 9:24	So for the second time they called the man who had been blind, and said to him, 'Give God the praise; we know that this man is a sinner.'
Jn 9:29	'. . . We know that God has spoken to Moses, but as for this man, we do not know where he comes from.'
Jn 10:19,20	There was again a division among the Jews because of these words. Many of them said, 'He has a demon, and he is mad; why listen to him?'
Mt. 9:34	But the Pharisees said, 'He casts out demons by the prince of demons.'
Mt. 12:24	But when the Pharisees heard it they said, 'It is only by Beelzebul, the prince of demons, that this man casts out demons.'
Jn 10:30-33	'I and the Father are one.' The Jews took up stones again to stone him. Jesus answered them, 'I have shown you many good works from the Father; for which of these do you stone me?' The Jews answered him, 'We stone you for no good work but for blasphemy; because you, being a man, make yourself God.'

Lk. 15:2	And the Pharisees and the scribes murmured, saying, 'This man receives sinners and eats with them.'
Lk. 16:14	The Pharisees, who were lovers of money, heard all this, and they scoffed at him.
Jn 11:47, 48	So the chief priests and the Pharisees gathered the council, and said, 'What are we to do? For this man performs many signs. If we let him go on thus, every one will believe in him, and the Romans will come and destroy both our holy place and our nation.'
Mt. 21:15	But when the chief priests and the scribes saw the wonderful things that he did, and the children crying out in the temple, 'Hosanna to the Son of David!' they were indignant . . . .
Lk. 19:47	And he was teaching daily in the temple. The chief priests and the scribes and the principal men of the people sought to destroy him;
Mk 11:28	. . . and they said to him, 'By what authority are you doing these things, or who gave you this authority to do them . . . .'
Mt. 21:45,46	When the chief priests and the Pharisees heard his parables, they perceived that he was speaking about them. But when they tried to arrest him, they feared the multitudes, because they held him to be a prophet.
Jn 15:20	'Remember the word that I said to you, "A servant is not greater than his master." If they persecuted me, they will persecute you; if they kept my word, they will keep yours also.'
Mk 14:45	And when he came, he went up to him at once, and said, 'Master'. And he kissed him.
Mk 14:48	And Jesus said to them, 'Have you come out as against a robber, with swords and clubs to capture me?'
Mt. 26:61	'This fellow said, "I am able to destroy the temple of God, and to build it in three days."'
Mt. 26:63	But Jesus was silent. And the high priest said to him, 'I adjure you by the living God, tell us if you are the Christ, the Son of God.'

Mt. 26:65,66	Then the high priest tore his robes, and said, 'He has uttered blasphemy. Why do we still need witnesses? You have now heard his blasphemy. What is your judgment?' They answered, 'He deserves death.'
Jn 18:29-31	So Pilate went out to them and said, 'What accusation do you bring against this man?' They answered him, 'If this man were not an evildoer, we would not have handed him over.' Pilate said to them, 'Take him yourselves and judge him by your own law.' The Jews said to him, 'It is not lawful for us to put any man to death.'
Lk. 23:11	And Herod with his soldiers treated him with contempt and mocked him; then, arraying him in gorgeous apparel, he sent him back to Pilate.
Lk. 23:18	But they all cried out together, 'Away with this man, and release to us Barabbas'
Jn 18:23	Jesus answered him, 'If I have spoken wrongly, bear witness to the wrong; but if I have spoken rightly, why do you strike me?'
Mk 15:18,19	And they began to salute him, 'Hail, King of the Jews.' And they struck his head with a reed, and spat upon him, and they knelt down in homage to him.
Jn 19:6,7	When the chief priests and the officers saw him, they cried out, 'Crucify him, crucify him.' Pilate said to them, 'Take him yourselves and crucify him, for I find no crime in him.' The Jews answered him, 'We have a law, and by that law he ought to die, because he has made himself the Son of God.'
Jn 19:15	They cried out, 'Away with him, away with him, crucify him.' Pilate said to them, 'Shall I crucify your King?' The chief priests answered 'We have no king but Caesar.'
Mt. 27:40-43	'You who would destroy the temple and build it in three days, save yourself! If you are the Son of God, come down from the cross.' So also the chief priests, with the scribes and elders, mocked him, saying, 'He saved others; he cannot save himself. He is the King of Israel; let him come down now from the cross, and we will

believe in him. He trusts in God; let God deliver him now, if he desires him; for he said, "I am the Son of God."'

Mk 15:32 '. . . Let the Christ, the King of Israel, come down now from the cross, that we may see and believe.' Those who were crucified with him also reviled him.

Lk. 23:39 One of the criminals who were hanged railed at him, saying, 'Are you not the Christ? Save yourself and us.'

Mt. 27:63 'Sir, we remember how that imposter said, while he was still alive, "After three days I will rise again."'

10. Faith

i. Lack of Faith is blameworthy

Lk. 1:20 — 'And behold, you will be silent and unable to speak until the day that these things come to pass, because you did not believe my words, which will be fulfilled in their time.'

Jn 3:32 — He bears witness to what he has seen and heard, yet no one receives his testimony . . . .

Jn 3:36 — He who believes in the Son has eternal life; he who does not obey the Son shall not see life, but the wrath of God rests upon him.

Jn 4:48 — Jesus therefore said to him, 'Unless you see signs and wonders you will not believe.'

Mt. 13:58 — And he did not do many mighty works there, because of their unbelief.

Mt. 14:31 — Jesus immediately reached out his hand and caught him, saying to him, 'O man of little faith, why did you doubt?'

Jn 6:65,66 — And he said, 'This is why I told you that no one can come to me unless it is granted him by the Father.' After this many of his disciples drew back and no longer went about with him.

Jn 5:38 — '. . . and you do not have his word abiding in you, for you do not believe him whom he has sent.'

Jn 5:44-47 — 'How can you believe, who receive glory from one another and do not seek the glory that comes from the only God? Do not think that I shall accuse you to the Father; it is Moses who accuses you, on whom you set your hope. If you believed Moses, you would believe me, for he wrote of me. But if you do not believe his writings, how will you believe my words?'

Mt. 16:4 — 'An evil and adulterous generation seeks for a sign, but no sign shall be given to it except the sign of Jonah.' So he left them and departed.

Mt. 16:8 — But Jesus, aware of this, said, 'O men of little faith, why do you discuss among yourselves the fact that you have no bread?'

Mk 9:19	And he answered them, 'O faithless generation, how long am I to be with you? Bring him to me.'
Mk 9:22,23	'And it has often cast him into the fire and into the water, to destroy him, but if you can do anything, have pity on us and help us.' And Jesus said to him, 'If you can! All things are possible to him who believes.'
Mt. 11:20-24	Then he began to upbraid the cities where most of his mighty works had been done, because they did not repent. 'Woe to you, Chorazin! woe to you, Bethsaida! for if the mighty works done in you had been done in Tyre and Sidon, they would have repented long ago in sackcloth and ashes. But I tell you, it shall be more tolerable on the day of judgment for Tyre and Sidon than for you. And you, Capernaum, will you be exalted to heaven? You shall be brought down to Hades. For if the mighty works done in you had been done in Sodom, it would have remained until this day. But I tell you that it shall be more tolerable on the day of judgment for the land of Sodom than for you.'
Jn 7:5	For even his brethren did not believe in him.
Jn 8:24	'I told you that you would die in your sins, for you will die in your sins unless you believe that I am he.'
Jn 8:44-47	'You are of your father the devil, and your will is to do your father's desires. He was a murderer from the beginning, and has nothing to do with the truth, because there is no truth in him. When he lies, he speaks according to his own nature, for he is a liar and the father of lies. But, because I tell you the truth, you do not believe me. Which of you convicts me of sin? If I tell you the truth, why do you not believe me? He who is of God hears the words of God; the reason why you do not hear them is that you are not of God.'
Lk. 16:31	He said to him, 'If they do not hear Moses and the prophets, neither will they be convinced if someone should rise from the dead.'
Lk. 18:7,8	'And will God not vindicate his elect, who cry to him day and night? Will he delay long over them? I tell you, he

will vindicate them speedily. Nevertheless, when the Son of man comes, will he find faith on earth?'

Mt. 21:32 'For John came to you in the way of righteousness, and you did not believe him, but the tax collectors and the harlots believed him: and even when you saw it, you did not afterward repent and believe him.'

Jn 12:37-43 Though he had done so many signs before them, yet they did not believe in him; it was that the word spoken by the prophet Isaiah might be fulfilled:
'Lord, who has believed our report,
and to whom has the arm of the Lord been revealed?'
Therefore they could not believe. For Isaiah again said,
'He has blinded their eyes and hardened their heart,
lest they should see with their eyes and perceive with their heart,
and turn to me to heal them.'
Isaiah said this because he saw his glory and spoke of him. Nevertheless many even of the authorities believed in him, but for fear of the Pharisees they did not confess it, lest they should be put out of the synagogue: for they loved the praise of men more than the praise of God.

Jn 16:8,9 'And when he comes, he will convince the world of sin and of righteousness and of judgment: of sin, because they do not believe in me . . . .'

Lk. 24:11 . . . but these words seemed to them an idle tale, and they did not believe them.

Mk 16:11 But when they heard that he was alive and had been seen by her, they would not believe it.

Lk. 24:25 And he said to them, 'O foolish men, and slow of heart to believe all that the prophets have spoken.'

Mk 16:14 Afterward he appeared to the eleven themselves as they sat at table; and he upbraided them for their unbelief and hardness of heart, because they had not believed those who saw him after he had risen.

Mt. 28:17 And when they saw him they worshipped him; but some doubted.

ii. Faith is praiseworthy

Lk. 1:45	'And blessed is she who believed that there would be a fulfilment of what was spoken to her from the Lord.'
Jn 3:14-16	'And as Moses lifted up the serpent in the wilderness, so must the Son of man be lifted up, that whoever believes in him may have eternal life.' For God so loved the world that he gave his only Son,. that whoever believes in him should not perish but have eternal life.
Jn 3:18	He who believes in him is not condemned, he who does not believe is condemned already, because he has not believed in the name of the only Son of God.
Jn 3:33,34	. . . he who receives his testimony sets his seal to this, that God is true. For he whom God has sent utters the words of God, for it is not by measure that he gives the Spirit . . . .
Jn 3:36	He who believes in the Son has eternal life; he who does not obey the Son shall not see life, but the wrath of God rests upon him.
Mt. 8:10	When Jesus heard him, he marvelled, and said to those who followed him, 'Truly, I say to you, not even in Israel have I found such faith.'
Mk 5:36	But ignoring what they had said, Jesus said to the ruler of the synagogue, 'Do not fear, only believe.'
Jn 6:29	Jesus answered them, 'This is the work of God, that you believe in him whom he has sent.'
Jn 6:35-37	Jesus said to them, 'I am the bread of life; he who comes to me shall not hunger, and he who believes in me shall never thirst. But I said to you that you have seen me and yet do not believe. All that the Father gives me will come to me; and him who comes to me I will not cast out.'
Jn 6:40	'For this is the will of my Father, that every one who sees the Son and believes in him should have eternal life; and I will raise him up at the last day.'
Jn 6:47	'Truly, truly, I say to you, he who believes has eternal life.'

Jn 5:24 'Truly, truly, I say to you, he who hears my word and believes him who sent me, has eternal life; he does not come into judgment, but has passed from death to life.'

Lk 17:6 And the Lord said, 'If you had faith as a grain of mustard seed, you could say to this sycamine tree, "Be rooted up, and be planted in the sea," and it would obey you.'

Jn 7:38 'He who believes in me, as the scripture has said, "Out of his heart shall flow rivers of living water."'

Jn 8:31,32 Jesus said to the Jews who had believed in him, 'If you continue in my word, you are truly my disciples, and you will know the truth, and the truth will make you free.'

Jn 9:35-38 Jesus heard that they had cast him out, and having found him he said, 'Do you believe in the Son of man?' He answered, 'And who is he, sir, that I might believe in him?' Jesus said to him, 'You have seen him, and it is he who speaks to you.' He said, 'Lord, I believe'; and he worshipped him.

Jn 11:25-27 Jesus said to her, 'I am the resurrection and the life, he who believes in me, though he die, yet shall he live, and whoever lives and believes in me shall never die. Do you believe this?' She said to him, 'Yes, Lord; I believe that you are the Christ, the Son of God, he who is coming into the world.'

Jn 11:40-42 Jesus said to her, 'Did I not tell you that if you would believe you would see the glory of God?' So they took away the stone. And Jesus lifted up his eyes and said, 'Father, I thank thee that thou hast heard me. I knew that thou hearest me always, but I have said this on account of the people standing by, that they might believe that thou didst send me.'

Jn 12:35,36 Jesus said to them, 'The light is with you for a little longer. Walk while you have the light, lest the darkness overtake you; he who walks in the darkness does not know where he goes. While you have the light believe in the light, that you may become sons of light.'

Jn 12:44-46 And Jesus cried out and said, 'He who believes in me, believes not in me, but in him who sent me. And he who sees me sees him who sent me. I have come as light into the world, that whoever believes in me may not remain in darkness.'

Jn 14:10 'Do you not believe that I am in the Father and the Father in me? The words that I say to you I do not speak on my own authority; but the Father who dwells in me does his works.'

Jn 17:20-22 'I do not pray for these only, but also for those who believe in me through their word, that they may all be one, even as thou, Father, art in me, and I in thee, that they also may be in us, that the world may believe that thou hast sent me. The glory which thou hast given me I have given to them, that they may be one, even as we are one.'

Jn 20:27-29 Then he said to Thomas, 'Put your fingers here, and see my hands; and put out your hand, and place it in my side, do not be faithless, but believing.' Thomas answered him, 'My Lord and my God.' Jesus said to him, 'Have you believed because you have seen me? Blessed are those who have not seen and yet believe.'

Mk 16:16 'He who believes and is baptized will be saved; but he who does not believe will be condemned.'

Jn 20:30,31 Now Jesus did many other signs in the presence of the disciples, which are not written in this book; but these are written that you may believe that Jesus is the Christ, the Son of God, and that believing you may have life in his name.

iii. Other motives for Faith

Jn 1:50 Jesus answered him, 'Because I said to you, I saw you under the fig tree, do you believe? You shall see greater things than these.'

Jn 2:23 Now when he was in Jerusalem at the Passover feast, many believed in his name when they saw the signs which he did . . . .

Jn 4:39 Many Samaritans from that city believed in him because of the woman's testimony, 'He told me all that I ever did.'

Jn 4:41,42 — And many more believed because of his word. They said to the woman, 'It is no longer because of your words that we believe, for we have heard for ourselves, and we know that this is indeed the Saviour of the world.'

Jn 4:48 — Jesus therefore said to him, 'Unless you see signs and wonders you will not believe.'

Mt. 11:4-6 — And Jesus answered them, 'Go and tell John what you hear and see; the blind receive their sight and the lame walk, lepers are cleansed and the deaf hear, and the dead are raised up, and the poor have good news preached to them. And blessed is he who takes no offence at me.'

Jn 5:36 — 'But the testimony which I have is greater than that of John; for the works which the Father has granted me to accomplish, these very works which I am doing, bear me witness that the Father has sent me.'

Jn 7:31 — Yet many of the people believed in him; they said, 'When the Christ appears, will he do more signs than this man has done?'

Jn 8:29,30 — 'And he who sent me is with me; he has not left me alone, for I always do what is pleasing to him.' As he spoke thus, many believed in him.

Mt. 13:16,17 — 'But blessed are your eyes, for they see, and your ears, for they hear. Truly, I say to you, many prophets and righteous men longed to see what you see, and did not see it, and to hear what you hear, and did not hear it.'

Jn 10:25 — Jesus answered them, 'I told you, and you do not believe. The works that I do in my Father's name, they bear witness to me . . . .'

Jn 10:37,38 — 'If I am not doing the works of my Father, then do not believe me; but if I do them, even though you do not believe me, believe the works, that you may know and understand that the Father is in me and I am in the Father.'

Jn 10:41,42 — And many came to him; and they said, 'John did no sign, but everything that John said about this man was true.' And many believed in him there.

Jn 11:47,48	So the chief priests and the Pharisees gathered the council, and said, 'What are we to do? For this man performs many signs. If we let him go on thus, every one will believe in him, and the Romans will come and destroy both our holy places and our nation.'
Jn 14:12	'Truly, truly, I say to you, he who believes in me will also do the works that I do and greater works than these will he do, because I go to the Father.'
Jn 20:8	Then the other disciple, who reached the tomb first, also went in, and he saw and believed. . . .
Mk 16:20	And they went forth and preached everywhere, while the Lord worked with them and confirmed the message by the signs that attended it. Amen.

iv. Examples and rewards of Faith

Jn 2:2-5	Jesus also was invited to the marriage, with his disciples. When the wine failed, the mother of Jesus said to him, 'They have no wine.' And Jesus said to her, 'O woman, what have you to do with me? My hour has not yet come.' His mother said to the servants, 'Do whatever he tells you.'
Jn 4:53	The father knew that was the hour when Jesus had said to him, 'Your son will live'; and he himself believed, and all his household.
Mt. 9:2	And behold they brought to him a paralytic, lying on his bed; and when Jesus saw their faith he said to the paralytic, 'Take heart, my son; your sins are forgiven.'
Lk. 8:15	And he said to the woman, 'Your faith has saved you; go in peace.'
Lk. 8:15	'And as for that in the good soil, they are those who, hearing the word, hold it fast in an honest and good heart, and bring forth fruit with patience.'
Mk 5:34	And he said to her, 'Daughter, your faith has made you well; go in peace, and be healed of your disease.'
Jn 6:69	'. . . and we have believed, and have come to know, that you are the Holy One of God.'

Mt. 15:28 — Then Jesus answered her, 'O woman, great is your faith! Be it done for you as you desire.' And her daughter was healed instantly.

Mt. 9:28,29 — And when he entered the house, the blind man came to him; and Jesus said to them, 'Do you believe that I am able to do this?' They said to him, 'Yes, Lord.' Then he touched their eyes, saying, 'According to your faith be it done to you.'

Lk. 18:28-30 — And Peter said, 'Lo, we have left our homes and followed you.' And he said to them, 'Truly, I say to you, there is no man who has left house or wife or brothers or parents or children, for the sake of the kingdom of God, who will not receive manifold more in this time, and in the age to come eternal life.'

Lk. 18:42 — And Jesus said to him, 'Receive your sight; your faith has made you well.'

Mt. 21:21,22 — And Jesus answered them, 'Truly, I say to you, if you have faith and never doubt, you will not only do what has been done to the fig tree, but even if you say to this mountain, "Be taken up and cast into the sea," it will be done. And whatever you ask in prayer, you will receive, if you have faith.'

Jn 14:12 — 'Truly, truly, I say to you, he who believes in me will also do the works that I do; and greater works than these will he do, because I go to the Father.'

Jn 16:27 — '. . . for the Father himself loves you, because you have loved me and have believed that I came from the Father.'

Lk. 24:31-34 — And their eyes were opened and they recognized him; and he vanished out of their sight. They said to each other, 'Did not our hearts burn within us while he talked to us on the road, while he opened to us the scriptures?' And they rose that same hour and returned to Jerusalem; and they found the eleven gathered together and those who were with them, who said, 'The Lord has risen indeed, and has appeared to Simon.'

11. Calls and Commissions

i. Preparatory Calls

Lk. 1:11-17

And there appeared to him an angel of the Lord standing on the right side of the altar of incense. And Zechariah was troubled when he saw him, and fear fell upon him. But the angel said to him, 'Do not be afraid, Zechariah, for your prayer is heard, and your wife Elizabeth will bear you a son, and you shall call his name John.

'And you will have joy and gladness,
and many will rejoice at his birth;
for he will be great before the Lord,
and he shall drink no wine
or strong drink,
and he will be filled with the Holy Spirit,
even from his mother's womb.
And he will turn many of the sons of Israel to the Lord their God,
and he will go before him in the spirit and power of Elijah,
to turn the hearts of the fathers to the children,
and the disobedient to the wisdom of the just,
to make ready for the Lord a people prepared.'

Lk. 1:28-38

And he came to her and said, 'Hail, full of grace, the Lord is with you!' But she was greatly troubled at the saying, and considered in her mind what sort of greeting this might be. And the angel said to her, 'Do not be afraid, Mary, for you have found favour with God. And behold, you will conceive in your womb, and bear a son, and you shall call his name Jesus.

'He will be great, and will be called the Son of the Most High;
and the Lord God will give to him the throne of his father David,
and he will reign over the house of Jacob for ever;
and of his kingdom there will be no end.'

And Mary said to the angel, 'How can this be, since I have no husband?' And the angel said to her,

'The Holy Spirit will come upon you,
and the power of the Most High will overshadow you;

therefore the child to be born will be called holy,
the Son of God.'

'And behold, your kinswoman Elizabeth in her old age has also conceived a son; and this is the sixth month with her who was called barren. For with God nothing is impossible.' And Mary said, 'Behold, I am the handmaid of the Lord; let it be to me according to your word.' And the angel departed from her.

Lk. 1:76 '. . . And you, child, will be called the prophet of the Most High . . . .'

Mt. 2:1,2 Now when Jesus was born in Bethlehem of Judea in the days of Herod the King, behold, wise men from the East came to Jerusalem, saying, 'Where is he who has been born king of the Jews? For we have seen his star in the East, and have come to worship him.'

Lk. 3:2,3 . . . in the high-priesthood of Annas and Caiaphas, the word of God came to John the son of Zechariah in the wilderness; and he went into all the region about the Jordan, preaching a baptism of repentance for the forgiveness of sins.

ii. Christ calls the Twelve

Jn 1:35-51 The next day again John was standing with two of his disciples; and he looked at Jesus as he walked, and said, 'Behold, the Lamb of God.' The two disciples heard him say this, and they followed Jesus. Jesus turned, and saw them following, and said to them, 'What do you seek?' And they said to him, 'Rabbi' (which means Teacher), 'where are you staying?' He said to them, 'Come and see.' They came and saw where he was staying; and they stayed with him that day for it was about the tenth hour. One of the two who heard John speak, and followed him, was Andrew. Simon Peter's brother. He first found his brother Simon, and said to him, 'We have found the Messiah' (which means Christ). He brought him to Jesus. Jesus looked at him, and said, 'So you are Simon the son of John? You shall be called Cephas' (which means Peter).

The next day Jesus decided to go to Galilee. And he

found Philip and said to him, 'Follow me.' Now Philip was from Bethsaida, the city of Andrew and Peter. Philip found Nathanael, and said to him, 'We have found him of whom Moses in the law and also the prophets wrote, Jesus of Nazareth, the son of Joseph.' Nathanael said to him, 'Can anything good come out of Nazareth?' Philip said to him, 'Come and see.' Jesus saw Nathanael coming to him, and said of him, 'Behold, an Israelite indeed, in whom is no guile.' Nathanael said to him, 'How do you know me?' Jesus answered him, 'Before Philip called you, when you were under the fig tree, I saw you.' Nathanael answered him, 'Rabbi, you are the Son of God. You are the King of Israel.' Jesus answered him, 'Because I said to you, I saw you under the fig tree, do you believe? You shall see greater things than these.' And he said to him, 'Truly, truly, I say to you, you will see heaven opened, and the angels of God ascending and descending upon the Son of man.'

Lk. 5:8-11 But when Simon Peter saw it, he fell down at Jesus' knees, saying, 'Depart from me, for I am a sinful man, O Lord.' For he was astonished, and all that were with him, at the catch of fish which they had taken; and so also were James and John, sons of Zebedee, who were partners with Simon. And Jesus said to Simon, 'Do not be afraid; henceforth you will be catching men.' And when they had brought their boats to land, they left everything and followed him.

Mt. 4:18-22 As he walked by the Sea of Galilee, he saw two brothers, Simon who is called Peter and Andrew his brother, casting a net into the sea; for they were fishermen. And he said to them, 'Follow me, and I will make you fishers of men.' Immediately they left their nets and followed him. And going on from there he saw two other brothers, James the son of Zebedee and his brother, in the boat with Zebedee their father, mending their nets, and he called them. Immediately they left the boat and their father, and followed him.

Lk. 5:27,28 After this he went out, and saw a tax collector, named Levi, sitting at the tax office; and he said to him, 'Follow me.' And he left everything, and rose and followed him.

Mk 3:13-19 And he went up into the hills, and called to him those whom he desired; and they came to him. And he appointed twelve, to be with him, and to be sent out to preach and have authority to cast out demons: Simon whom he surnamed Peter; James the son of Zebedee and John the brother of James, whom he named Boanerges, that is, sons of thunder; Andrew and Philip, and Bartholomew, and Matthew, and Thomas, and James the son of Alphaeus, and Thaddeus, and Simon the Cananaean, and Judas Iscariot, who betrayed him.

iii. Commissions to members of the Twelve

Lk. 5:9,10 For he was astonished, and all that were with him, at the catch of fish which they had taken; and so also were James and John, sons of Zebedee,, who were partners with Simon. And Jesus said to Simon, 'Do not be afraid; henceforth you will be catching men.'

Mk 6:7 And he called to him the twelve, and began to send them out two by two, and gave them authority over the unclean spirits.

Lk. 9:28 Now about eight days after these sayings he took with him Peter and John and James, and went up on the mountain to pray.

Lk. 10:1 After this the Lord appointed seventy others, and sent them on ahead of him, two by two, into every town and place where he himself was about to come.

Mt. 16:17-19 And Jesus answered him, 'Blessed are you, Simon Bar-Jona. For flesh and blood has not revealed this to you, but my Father who is in heaven. And I tell you, you are Peter, and on this rock I will build my church, and the powers of death shall not prevail against it. I will give you the keys of the kingdom of heaven, and whatever you bind on earth shall be bound in heaven, and whatever you loose on earth shall be loosed in heaven.'

Mt. 19:27-30 Then Peter said in reply, 'Lo, we have left everything and followed you. What then shall we have?' Jesus said to them, 'Truly, I say to you, in the new world, when the

Son of man shall sit on his glorious throne, you who have followed men will also sit on twelve thrones, judging the twelve tribes of Israel. And every one who has left houses or brothers or sisters or father or mother or children or lands, for my name's sake, will receive a hundredfold, and inherit eternal life. But many that are first will be last, and the last first.'

Jn 12:6 This he said, not that he cared for the poor but because he was a thief, and as he had the money box he used to take what was put into it.

Lk. 22:31,32 'Simon, Simon, behold, Satan demanded to have you, that he might sift you like wheat, but I have prayed for you that your faith may not fail; and when you have turned again, strengthen your brethren.'

Mt. 26:37,38 And taking with him Peter and the two sons of Zebedee, he began to be sorrowful and troubled. Then he said to them, 'My soul is very sorrowful, even to death; remain here, and watch with me.' And going a little farther he fell on his face and prayed, 'My Father, if it be possible, let this cup pass from me; nevertheless, not as I will, but as thou wilt.'

Jn 19:25-27 But standing by the cross of Jesus were his mother, and his mother's sister, Mary the wife of Clopas, and Mary Magdalene. When Jesus saw his mother, and the disciple whom he loved standing near, he said to his mother, 'Woman, behold, your son'. Then he said to the disciple, 'Behold, your mother.' And from that hour the disciple took her to his own home.

Jn 20:21,23 Jesus said to them again, 'Peace be with you. As the Father has sent me, even so I send you.' And when he had said this, he breathed on them, and said to them, 'Receive the Holy Spirit. If you forgive the sins of any, they are forgiven; if you retain the sins of any, they are retained.'

Jn 20:27,28 Then he said to Thomas, 'Put your finger here, and see my hands; and put out your hand, and place it in my side; do not be faithless, but believing.' Thomas answered him, 'My Lord and my God!'

Jn 21:15-17 When they had finished breakfast, Jesus said to Simon Peter, 'Simon, son of John, do you love me more than these?' He said to him, 'Yes, Lord; you know that I love you.' He said to him, 'Feed my lambs.' A second time he said to him, 'Simon, son of John, do you love me?' He said to him, 'Yes, Lord; you know that I love you.' He said to him, 'Tend my sheep.' He said to him the third time, 'Simon, son of John, do you love me?' Peter was grieved because he said to him the third time, 'Do you love me?' And he said to him, 'Lord, you know everything; you know that I love you.' Jesus said to him, 'Feed my sheep.'

Mt. 28:18-20 And Jesus came and said to them, 'All authority in heaven and earth has been given to me. Go therefore and make disciples of all nations, baptizing them in the name of the Father and of the Son and of the Holy Spirit, teaching them to observe all that I have commanded you; and lo, I am with you always, to the close of the age.'

Lk. 24:48,49 '. . . You are witnesses of these things. And behold, I send the promise of my Father upon you; but stay in the city, until you are clothed with power from on high.'

iv. Other Commissions or Calls

Jn 2:5 His mother said to the servants, 'Do whatever he tells you.'

Mt. 11:4 And Jesus answered them, 'Go and tell John what you hear and see:

Lk. 8:1-3 Soon afterwards he went on through cities and villages, preaching and bringing the good news of the kingdom of God. And the twelve were with him, and also some women who had been healed of evil spirits and infirmities: Mary, called Magdalene, from whom seven demons had gone out, and Joanna, the wife of Chuza, Herod's steward, and Susanna, and many others, who provided for them out of their means.

Lk. 8:38,39 The man from whom the demons had gone begged that he might be with him; but he sent him away, saying, 'Return to your home, and declare how much God has done for you.' And he went away, proclaiming throughout the whole city how much Jesus had done for him.

Mk 5:18-20 And as he was getting into the boat, the man who had been possessed with demons begged him that he might be with him. But he refused, and said to him, 'Go home to your friends, and tell them how much the Lord has done for you, and how he has had mercy on you.' And he went away and began to proclaim in the Decapolis how much Jesus had done for him; and all men marvelled.

Mt. 28:7,8 '. . . Then go quickly and tell his disciples that he has risen from the dead, and behold, he is going before you to Galilee; there you will see him. Lo, I have told you.' So they departed quickly from the tomb with fear and great joy, and ran to tell his disciples.

Lk. 24:10 Now it was Mary Magdalene and Joanna and Mary the mother of James and the other women with them who told this to the apostles . . . .

Jn 20:17 Jesus said to her, 'Do not hold me, for I have not yet ascended to the Father; but go to my brethren and say to them, I am ascending to my Father and your Father, to my God and your God.'

Mt. 28:10 Then Jesus said to them 'Do not be afraid; go and tell my brethren to go to Galilee, and there they will see me.'

Lk. 24:33-35 And they rose that same hour and returned to Jerusalem; and they found the eleven gathered together and those who were with them, who said, 'The Lord has risen indeed, and has appeared to Simon.' Then they told what had happened on the road, and how he was known to them in the breaking of bread.

v. Unanswered Calls

Jn 6:70,71 Jesus answered them, 'Did I not choose you, the twelve, and one of you is a devil?' He spoke of Judas the son of Simon Iscariot, for he, one of the twelve, was to betray him.

Lk. 9:57-62 As they were going along the road, a man said to him, 'I will follow you wherever you go'. And Jesus said to him,

'Foxes have holes, and birds of the air have nests; but the Son of man has nowhere to lay his head.' To another he said, 'Follow me.' But he said, 'Lord, let me first go and bury my father.' But he said to him, 'leave the dead to bury their own dead; but as for you, go and proclaim the kingdom of God.' Another said, 'I will follow you, Lord: but let me first say farewell to those at my home.' Jesus said to him, 'No one who puts his hand to the plough and looks back is fit for the kingdom of God.'

Mk 10:21,22 And Jesus looking upon him loved him, and said to him, 'You lack one thing; go, sell what you have, and give to the poor, and you will have treasure in heaven; and come, follow me.' At that saying his countenance fell, and he went away sorrowful; for he had great possessions.

Jn 19:38 After this Joseph of Arimathea, who was a disciple of Jesus, but secretly, for fear of the Jews, asked Pilate that he might take away the body of Jesus, and Pilate gave him leave.

12. Compassion

i. God's compassion

Jn 3:16	For God so loved the world that he gave his only Son, that whoever believes in him should not perish but have eternal life.
Mt. 12:7	And if you had known what this means, 'I desire mercy, and not sacrifice,' you would not have condemned the guiltless.
Mt. 6:8	'Do not be like them, for your Father knows what you need before you ask him.'
Lk. 15:31,32	And he said to him, 'Son, you are always with me, and all that is mine is yours. It was fitting to make merry and be glad, for this your brother was dead, and is alive; he was lost, and is found.'
Lk. 18:7	And will not God vindicate his elect, who cry to him day and night? Will he delay long over them?'

ii. Christ's compassion

Lk. 4:17-19	And there was given to him the book of the prophet Isaiah. He opened the book and found the place where it was written, 'The Spirit of the Lord is upon me, because he has anointed me to reach good news to the poor. He has sent me to proclaim release to the captives and recovering of sight to the blind, to set at liberty those who are oppressed, to proclaim the acceptable year of the Lord.'
Mt. 12:19-21	'He will not wrangle or cry aloud, nor will anyone hear his voice in the streets; he will not break a bruised reed or quench a smouldering wick till he brings justice to victory; and in his name will the Gentiles hope.'
Lk. 7:22	And he answered them, 'Go and tell John what you have seen and heard; the blind receive their sight, the lame walk, lepers are cleansed, and the deaf hear, the dead are raised up, the poor have good news preached to them.
Mt. 9:36-38	When he saw the crowds, he had compassion for them, because they were harassed and helpless, like sheep

without a shepherd. Then he said to his disciples, 'The harvest is plentiful, but the labourers are few; pray therefore the Lord of the harvest to send out labourers into his harvest.'

Mk 6:34 As he landed he saw a great throng and he had compassion on them, because they were like sheep without a shepherd; and he began to teach them many things.

Mt. 15:32 Then Jesus called his disciples to him and said, 'I have compassion on the crows, because they have been with me now three days, and have nothing to eat; and I am unwilling to send them away hungry, lest they faint on the way.'

Mk 9:35-37 And he sat down and called the twelve; and he said to them, 'If anyone would be first, he must be last of all and servant of all'. And he took a child, and put him in the midst of them; and taking him in his arms, he said to them, 'Whoever receives one such child in my name receives me; and whoever receives me, receives not me but him who sent me.'

Mt. 10:42 'And whoever gives to me of these little ones even a cup of cold water because he is a disciple, truly, I say, to you, he shall not lose his reward.'

Mt. 18:5 'Whoever receives one such child in my name, receives me . . . .'

Lk. 9:53-56 But the people would not receive him because his face was set toward Jerusalem. And when his disciples James and John saw it, they said, 'Lord, do you want us to bid fire come down from heaven and consume them?' But he turned and rebuked them. And they went on to another village.

Mt. 11:28,29 'Come to me, all who labour and are heavy laden, and I will give you rest. Take my yoke upon you, and learn from me; for I am gentle and lowly in heart, and you will find rest for your souls.'

Lk. 10:36,37 'Which of these three, do you think, proved neighbour to the man who fell among the robbers?' He said, 'The one who showed mercy on him.' And Jesus said to him, 'Go and do likewise.'

Mt. 7:7,12 'Ask, and it will be given you; seek, and you will find; knock, and it will be opened to you. For everyone who asks receives, and he who seeks finds, and to him who knocks it will be opened. Or what man of you, if his son asks him for bread, will he give him a stone? Or if he asks for a fish, will he give him a serpent? If you then, who are evil, know how to give good gifts to your children, how much more will your Father who is in heaven give good things to those who ask him. So whatever you wish that men would do to you, do so to them; for this is the law and the prophets.'

Lk. 14:23,24 And the master said to the servant, 'Go out to the highways and hedges, and compel people to come in, that my house may be filled. For I tell you, none of these men who were invited shall taste my banquet.'

Mk 11:25,26 'And whenever you stand praying, forgive, if you have anything against any one; so that your Father also who is in heaven may forgive you your trespasses.'

Lk. 22:15 And he said to them, 'I have earnestly desired to eat this passover with you before I suffer.'

Mk 12:43,44 'Truly I say to you, this poor widow has put in more than all those who are contributing to the treasury. For they all contributed out of their abundance; but she out of her poverty has put in everything she had, her whole living.'

Mt. 25:40 And the King will answer them, 'Truly, I say to you, as you did it to one of the least of these my brethren, you did it to me.'

Jn 13:14, 15 'If I then, your Lord and Teacher, have washed your feet, you also ought to wash one another's feet. For I have given you an example, that you also should do as I have done to you.'

Jn 13:34,35 'A new commandment I give to you, that you love one another, even as I have loved you, that you also love one another. By this all men will know that you are my disciples, if you have love for one another.'

Jn 15:9 'As the Father has loved me, so have I loved you; abide in my love.'

Jn 15:12,13 'This is my commandment, that you love one another as I have loved you. Greater love has no man than this, that a man lay down his life for his friends.'

Mt. 26:52,55 Then Jesus said to him, 'Put your sword back into its place; for all who take the sword will perish by the sword. Do you think that I cannot appeal to my Father, and he will at once send me more than twelve legions of angels? But how then should the scriptures be fulfilled, that it must be so?' At that hour Jesus said to the crowds, 'Have you come out as against a robber, with swords and clubs to capture me? Day after day I sat in the temple teaching, and you did not seize me.'

Lk. 23:28 But Jesus turning to them said, 'Daughters of Jerusalem, do not weep for me, but weep for yourselves and for your children.'

Jn 19:26-27 When Jesus saw his mother, and the disciple whom he loved standing near, he said to his mother, 'Woman, behold, your son.' Then he said to the disciple, 'Behold your Mother.' And from that hour the disciple took her to his own home.

Lk. 23:42-43 And he said, 'Jesus, remember me when you come in your kingly power.' And he said to him, 'Truly, I say to you, today you will be with me in Paradise.'

iii. Forgiveness and compassion

Mt. 5:23 'So if you are offering your gift at the altar, and there remember that your brother has something against you, leave your gift there before the altar and go; first be reconciled to your brother, and then come and offer your gift.'

Mt. 5:38-48 'You have heard that it was said, "An eye for an eye and a tooth for a tooth." But I say to you, Do not resist one who is evil. But if any one strikes you on the cheek, turn to him the other also; and if any one would sue you and take your coat, let him have your cloak as well, and if any one forces you to go one mile, go with him two miles. Give to him who begs from you, and do not refuse him who would borrow from you.

'You have heard that it was said, "You shall love your

neighbour and hate your enemy," But I say to you, Love your enemies and pray for those who persecute you, so that you may be the sons of your Father who is in heaven; For he makes his sun rise on the evil and on the good, and send rain on the just and on the unjust. For if you love those who love you, what reward have you? Do not even the tax collectors do the same? And if you salute only your brethren what more are you doing than others? Do not even the Gentiles do the same? You, therefore, must be perfect as your heavenly Father is perfect.'

Mt. 7:12 'So whatever you wish that men would do to you, do so to them; for this is the law and the prophets.'

Lk. 6:35-42 'But love your enemies, and do good and lend, expecting nothing in return; and your reward will be great, and you will be sons of the Most High; for he is kind to the ungrateful and the selfish. Be merciful as your Father is merciful.

'Judge not, and you will not be judged; condemn not, and you will not be condemned; forgive and you will be forgiven; give, and it will be given to you; good measure, pressed down, shaken together, running over, will be put into your lap. For the measure you give will be the measure you get back.'

He also told them a parable: 'Can a blind man lead a blind man? Will they not both fall into a pit? A disciple is not above his Teacher, but every one when he is fully taught will be like his teacher. Why do you see the speck that is in your brother's eye, but do not notice the log that is in your own eye? Or how can you say to your brother, "Brother, let me take out the speck that is in your eye," when you yourself do not see the log that is in your own eye? You hypocrite, first take the log out of your own eye, and then you will see clearly to take out the speck that is in your brother's eye.'

Mt. 10:8 'Heal the sick, raise the dead, cleanse lepers, cast out demons. You received without pay, give without pay.'

Mt. 18:6 '. . . but whoever causes one of these little ones who believe in me to sin, it would be better for him to have a great millstone fastened round his neck and to be drowned in the depth of the sea.'

Mt. 18:21,22 Then Peter came up and said to him, 'Lord, how often shall my brother sin against me, and I forgive him? As many as seven times?' Jesus said to him, 'I do not say to you seven times, but seventy times seven.'

Mt. 18:32,33 Then his Lord summoned him and said to him, 'You wicked servant. I forgave you all that debt because you besought me; and should not you have had mercy on your fellow servant, as I had mercy on you?'

Jn 10:12,13 'He who is a hireling and not a shepherd, whose own the sheep are not, sees the wolf coming and leaves the sheep and flees; and the wolf snatches them and scatters them. He flees because he is a hireling and cares nothing for the sheep.'

Mt. 6:11-15 'Give us this day our daily bread; and forgive us our debts, as we also have forgiven our debtors; and lead us not into temptation, but deliver us from evil. For if you forgive men their trespasses, your heavenly Father also will forgive you, but if you do not forgive men their trespasses, neither will your Father forgive your trespasses.'

Mk 11:25,26 'And whenever you stand praying, forgive, if you have anything against anyone; so that your Father also who is in Heaven may forgive you your trespasses.'

Lk. 10:33-37 'But a Samaritan, as he journeyed, came to where he was; and when he saw him, he had compassion, and went up to him and bound up his wounds, pouring on oil and wine; then he set him on his own beast and brought him to an inn, and took care of him. And the next day he took out two denarii and gave them to the innkeeper, saying, "Take care of him; and whatever more you spend, I will repay you when I come back." Which of these three, do you think, proved neighbour to the man who fell among the robbers?' he said, 'The one who showed mercy on him.' And Jesus said to him, 'Go and do likewise.'

Lk. 11:46 And he said, 'Woe to you lawyers also. For you load men with burdens hard to bear, and you yourselves do not touch the burden with one of your fingers.'

Lk. 14:12-14 He said also to the man who had invited him, 'When you give a dinner or a banquet, do not invite your friends or your brothers or your kinsmen or rich neighbours, lest they also invite you in return, and you be repaid. But when you give a feast, invite the poor, the maimed, the lame, the blind, and you will be blessed, because they cannot repay you. You will be repaid at the resurrection of the just.'

Lk. 15:20-24 But while he was yet at a distance, his father saw him and had compassion, and ran and embraced him and kissed him. And the son said to him, 'Father, I have sinned against heaven and before you; I am no longer worthy to be called your son.' But the father said to his servants, 'Bring quickly the best robe, and put it on him; and put a ring on his hand, and shoes on his feet; and bring the fatted calf and kill it; and let us eat and make merry; for this my son was dead, and is alive again; he was lost, and is found.' And they began to make merry.

Mt. 25:45 Then he will answer them, 'Truly, I say to you, as you did it not to one of the least of these, you did it not to me.'

iv. Compassion shown to Christ

Jn 4:31 Meanwhile the disciples besought him, saying, 'Rabbi, eat.'

Lk. 10:41,42 But the Lord answered her, 'Martha, Martha, you are anxious and troubled about many things; one thing is needful. Mary has chosen the good portion, which shall not be taken away from her.'

Jn 11:16 Thomas, called the Twin, said to his fellow disciples, 'Let us also go, that we may die with him.'

Jn 12:3-8 Mary took a pound of costly ointment of pure nard and anointed the feet of Jesus and wiped his feet with her hair; and the house was filled with the fragrance of the ointment. But Judas Iscariot, one of his disciples (he who was to betray him), said, 'Why was this ointment not sold for three hundred denarii and given to the poor?' This he said, not that he cared for the poor but because he was a thief, and as he had the money box he used to take what was put into it. Jesus said, 'Let her alone, let her keep it for the day of my burial. The poor you have always with you, but you do not always have me.'

Lk. 23:27 And there followed him a great multitude of the people, and of women who bewailed and lamented him.

Lk. 23:40,41 But the other rebuked him, saying, 'Do you not fear God, since you are under the same sentence of condemnation? And we indeed justly; for we are receiving the due reward of our deeds; but this man has done nothing wrong.'

Jn 19:28,29 After this Jesus, knowing that all was now finished, said (to fulfil the scripture), 'I thirst.' A bowl full of vinegar stood there; so they put a sponge full of vinegar on hyssop and held it to his mouth . . . .

Lk. 23:50-52 Now there was a man named Joseph from the Jewish town of Arimathea, who was a disciple of Jesus, but secretly, for fear of the Jews, asked Pilate that he might take away the body of Jesus, and Pilate gave him leave. So he came and took away his body. Nicodemus also, who had at first come to him by night, came bringing a mixture of myrrh and aloes, about a hundred pounds' weight. They took the body of Jesus, and bound it in linen cloths with the spices, as is the burial custom of the Jews. Now in the place where he was crucified there was a garden, and in the garden a new tomb where no one had ever been laid.

Mk 16:1 And when the sabbath was past, Mary Magdalene, and Mary the mother of James, and Salome, brought spices, so that they might go and anoint him.

v. Compassion of men to others

Jn 2:3-5 When the wine failed, the mother of Jesus said to him, 'They have no wine.' And Jesus said to her, 'O woman, what have you to do with me? My hour has not yet come.' His mother said to the servants, 'Do whatever he tells you.'

Mt. 14:12	And his disciples came and took the body and buried it; and they went and told Jesus.
Lk. 19:8	And Zacchaeus stood and said to the Lord, 'Behold, Lord, the half of my goods I give to the poor; and if I have defrauded any one of anything, I restore it fourfold.'
Mk 12:41-44	And he sat down opposite the treasury, and watched the multitude putting money into the treasury. Many people put in large sums. And a poor widow came, and put in two copper coins, which make a penny. And he called his disciples to him, and said to them, 'Truly, I say to you, this poor widow has put in more than all those who are contributing to the treasury. For they all contributed out of their abundance; but she out of her poverty has put in everything she had, her whole living.'

See also: 3. vii. Salvation, forgiveness, mercy, redemption.

13. The Qualities Christ Demands: I

i. Reverence to the Father

Mt. 4:7	Jesus said to him, 'Again it is written, "You shall not tempt the Lord your God."'
Mt. 4:10	Then Jesus said to him, 'Begone, Satan! for it is written, "You shall worship the Lord your God and Him only shall you serve."'
Jn 2:16	And he told those who sold the pigeons, 'Take these things away; you shall not make my Father's house a house of trade.'
Mk 11:17	And he taught, and said to them, 'Is it not written, "My house shall be called a house of prayer for all the nations"? But you have made it a den of robbers.'
Mt. 7:6	'Do not give dogs what is holy; and do not throw your pearls before swine, lest they trample them under foot and turn to attack you.'
Jn 5:37	'And the Father who sent me has himself borne witness to me. His voice you have never heard, his form you have never seen.'
Mk 12:29,30	Jesus answered, 'The first is, "Hear, O Israel: the Lord our God, the Lord is one; and you shall love the Lord your God with all your heart, and with all your soul, and with all your mind, and with all your strength."'
Mt. 22:11,14	'But when the king came in to look at the guests, he saw there a man who had no wedding garment; and he said to him, "Friend, how did you get in here without a wedding garment?" And he was speechless. Then the king said to the attendants, "Bind him hand and foot, and cast him into the outer darkness; there men will weep and gnash their teeth. For many are called, but few are chosen."'
Lk. 16:13	'No servant can serve two masters; for either he will hate the one and love the other, or he will be devoted to the one and despise the other. You cannot serve God and mammon.'

Lk. 17:17,18 Then said Jesus, 'Were not ten cleansed? Where are the nine? Was no one found to return and give praise to God except this foreigner?'

ii. Reverence to Christ himself

Mt. 1:21 'She will bear a son, and you shall call his name Jesus, for he will save his people from their sins.'

Lk. 2:29-30 'Lord, now lettest thou thy servant depart in peace, according to thy word;
for mine eyes have seen thy salvation.'

Mt. 2:11 And going into the house they saw the child with Mary his mother, and they fell down and worshipped him. Then, opening their treasures, they offered him gifts of gold and frankincense and myrrh.

Lk. 3:16 John answered them all. 'I baptize you with water; but he who is mightier than I is coming, the thong of whose sandal I am not worthy to untie; he will baptize you with the Holy Spirit and with fire.'

Mt. 12:6 'I tell you something greater than the temple is here.'

Mt. 12:8 'For the Son of man is Lord of the sabbath.'

Lk. 7:26-28 'What then did you go out to see? A prophet? Yes, I tell you, and more than a prophet. This is he of whom it is written, "Behold I send my messenger before thy face, who shall prepare the way before thee." I tell you, among those born of women none is greater than John; yet he who is least in the kingdom of God is greater than he.'

Lk. 7:44-48 Then turning toward the woman he said to Simon, 'Do you see this woman? I entered your house, you gave me no water for my feet, but she has wet my feet with her tears and wiped them with her hair. You gave me no kiss, but from the time I came in she has not ceased to kiss my feet. You did not anoint my head with oil, but she has anointed my feet with ointment. Therefore I tell you, her sins, which are many, are forgiven for she loved much: But he who is forgiven little loves little.'

Mt. 13:37-38 He answered, 'He who sows the good seed is the Son of man; the field is the world, and the good seed means the sons of the kingdom; the weeds are the sons of the evil one.'

Lk. 4:24 'Truly, I say to you, no prophet is acceptable in his own country.'

Mt. 10:14,15 'And if anyone will not receive you or listen to your words, shake off the dust from your feet as you leave that house or town. Truly, I say to you, it shall be more tolerable on the day of judgment for the land of Sodom and Gomorrah than for that town.'

Jn 6:67-69 Jesus said to the twelve, 'Will you also go away?' Simon Peter answered him, 'Lord, to whom shall we go? You have the words of eternal life; and we have believed, and have come to know, that you are the Holy one of God.'

Mt. 16:15-17 He said to them: 'But who do you say that I am?' Simon Peter replied, 'You are the Christ, the Son of the living God.' And Jesus answered him, 'Blessed are you, Simon Bar-Jona. For flesh and blood has not revealed this to you, but my Father who is in heaven.'

Mt. 16: 24,25 Then Jesus told his disciples, 'If any man would come after me, let him deny himself and take up his cross and follow me. For whoever would save his life will lose it, and whoever loses his life for my sake will find it.'

Mk 8:38 'For whoever is ashamed of me and of my words in this adulterous and sinful generation, of him will the Son of man also be ashamed, when he comes in the glory of his Father with the holy angels.'

Mk 9:39-41 But Jesus said, 'Do not forbid him; for no one who does a mighty work in my name will be able soon after to speak evil of me. For he that is not against us is for us. For truly, I say to you, whoever gives you a cup of water to drink because you bear the name of Christ, will by no means lose his reward.'

Mt. 18:5 'Whoever receives one such child in my name receives me . . . .'

Jn 8:19	They said to him therefore; 'Where is your Father?' Jesus answered, 'You know neither me nor my Father: if you knew me, you would know my Father also.'
Jn 8:23	He said to them, 'You are from below, I am from above; you are of this world, I am not of this world.'
Jn 8:42	Jesus said to them, 'If God were your Father, you would love me, for I proceeded and come forth from God; I came not of my own accord, but he sent me.'
Lk. 9:59-62	To another he said, 'Follow me.' But he said, 'Lord, let me first go and bury my father.' But he said to him, 'Leave the dead to bury their own dead, but as for you, go and proclaim the kingdom of God.' Another said, 'I will follow you, Lord; but let me first say farewell to those at my home.' Jesus said to him, 'No one who puts his hand to the plough and looks back is fit for the kingdom of God.'
Lk. 10:10-12	But whenever you enter a town and they do not receive you, go into its streets and say, 'Even the dust of your town that clings to our feet, we wipe off against you; nevertheless know this, that the kingdom of God has come near.' I tell you, it shall be more tolerable on that day for Sodom than for that town.
Lk. 10:16	'He who hears you hears me, and he who rejects you rejects me, and he who rejects me rejects him who sent me.'
Mk 12:29,30	Jesus answered, 'The first is, Hear, O Israel: The Lord our God, the Lord is one; and you shall love the Lord your God with all your heart, and with all your soul, and with all your mind, and with all your strength.'
Lk. 11:23	'He who is not with me is against me, and he who does not gather with me scatters.'
Mk 3:28-30	'Truly, I say to you, all sins will be forgiven the sons of men, and whatever blasphemies they utter; but whoever blasphemes against the Holy Spirit never has forgiveness, but is guilty of an eternal sin' – for they had said, 'He has an unclean spirit.'
Lk. 12:8,9	'And I tell you, everyone who acknowledges me before men, the Son of man also will acknowledge before the

angels of God; but he who denies me before men will be denied before the angels of God.'

Lk. 12:37 'Blessed are those servants whom the master finds awake when he comes; truly, I say to you, he will gird himself and have them sit at table, and he will come and serve them.'

Mt. 10:34-36 'Do not think that I have come to bring peace on earth; I have not come to bring peace, but a sword. For I have come to set a man against his father, and a daughter against her mother, and a daughter-in-law against her mother-in-law; and a man's foes will be those of his own household.'

Mt. 22:7,8 The king was angry, and he sent his troops and destroyed those murderers and burned their city. Then he said to his servants, 'The wedding is ready, but those invited were not worthy.'

Lk. 14:26-27 'If any one comes to me and does not hate his own father and mother and wife and children and brothers and sisters, yes, and even his own life, he cannot be my disciple. Whoever does not bear his own cross and come after me, cannot be my disciple.'

Lk. 14:33 'So therefore, whoever of you does not renounce all that he has cannot be my disciple.'

Lk. 17:17-18 Then Jesus said, 'Were not ten cleansed? Where are the nine? Was no one found to return and give praise to God except this foreigner?'

Mk 10:21 And Jesus looking upon him loved him, and said to him, 'You lack one thing; go, sell what you have, and give to the poor, and you will have treasure in heaven; and come, follow me.'

Mt. 19:28-29 Jesus said to them, 'Truly, I say to you, in the new world, when the Son of Man shall sit on his glorious throne, you who have followed me will also sit on twelve thrones, judging the twelve tribes of Israel, and every one who has left houses or brothers or sisters or father or mother, or children or lands, for my name's sake, will receive a hundred fold, and inherit eternal life.'

Jn 11:16	Thomas called Twin, said to his fellow disciples, 'Let us also go, that we may die with him.'
Jn 11:25-26	Jesus said to her, 'I am the resurrection and the life; he who believes in me, though he die, yet shall he live, and whoever lives and believes in me shall never die. Do you believe this?'
Jn 12:3-8	Mary took a pound of costly ointment of pure nard and anointed the feet of Jesus and wiped his feet with her hair, and the house was filled with the fragrance of the ointment. But Judas Iscariot, one of his disciples (he who was to betray him), said, 'Why was this ointment not sold for three hundred denarii and given to the poor?' This he said, not that he cared for the poor but because he was a thief, and as he had the money box he used to take what was put into it. Jesus said, 'Let her alone, let her keep it for the day of my burial. The poor you always have with you, but you do not always have me.'
Mt. 26:12-13	'In pouring this ointment on my body she has done it to prepare me for burial. Truly, I say to you, wherever this gospel is preached in the whole world, what she has done will be told in memory of her.'
Mk 11:3	If anyone says to you, 'Why are you doing this?' say, 'The Lord has need of it and will send it back here immediately.'
Lk. 19:39-40	And some of the Pharisees in the multitude said to him, 'Teacher, rebuke your disciples.' He answered, 'I tell you, if these were silent, the very stones would cry out.'
Mt. 21:16	And they said to him, 'Do you hear what these are saying?' And Jesus said to them, 'Yes; have you never read "Out of the mouth of babes and sucklings thou hast brought perfect praise?"'
Jn 12:26	'If anyone serves me, he must follow me; and where I am, there shall my servant be also; if any one serves me, the Father will honour him.'
Mk 11:12-14	On the following day, when they came from Bethany, he was hungry. And seeing in the distance a fig tree in leaf, he went to see if he could find anything on it. When he came to it, he found nothing but leaves, for it was not the

season for figs. And he said to it, 'May no one ever eat fruit from you again.' And his disciples heard it.

Mt. 21:40-41 When therefore the owner of the vineyard comes, what will he do to those tenants?' They said to him, 'He will put those wretches to a miserable death, and let out the vineyards to other tenants who will give him the fruits in their seasons.'

Mt. 22:17,18 'Tell us, then, what you think. Is it lawful to pay taxes to Caesar, or not?' But Jesus, aware of their malice, said, 'Why put me to the test, you hypocrites?'

Mt. 22:41-44 Now while the Pharisees were gathered together, Jesus asked them a question, saying, 'What do you think of the Christ? Whose son is he?' They said to him, 'The son of David.' He said to them, 'How is it then that David, inspired by the Spirit, calls him Lord, saying, "The Lord said to my Lord, Sit at my right hand, till I put thy enemies under thy feet"?'

Lk. 21:23 'Heaven and earth will pass away, but my words will not pass away.'

Jn 13:13 'You call me Teacher and Lord; and you are right, for so I am.'

Jn 13:20 'Truly, truly, I say to you, he who receives any one whom I send receives me; and he who receives me receives him who sent me.'

Jn 14:9 Jesus said to him, 'Have I been with you so long, and yet you do not know me, Philip? He who has seen me has seen the Father; how can you say, "Show us the Father"?'

Jn 14:21 'He who has my commandments and keeps them, he it is who loves me; and he who loves me will be loved by my Father, and I will love him and manifest myself to him.'

Jn 15:23 'He who hates me hates my Father also.'

iii. Truthfulness and Integrity

Jn 1:47 Jesus saw Nathanael coming to him and said of him, 'Behold an Israelite indeed, in whom is no guile.'

Jn 3:16	For God so loved the world that he gave His only Son, that whoever believes in him should not perish but have eternal life.
Mk 8:15	And he cautioned them saying, 'Take heed, beware of the leaven of the Pharisees and the leaven of Herod.'
Mk 9:42-47	'Whoever causes one of these little ones who believe in me to sin, it would be better for him if a great millstone were hung round his neck and he were thrown into the sea. And if your hand causes you to sin, cut it off; it is better for you to enter life maimed than with two hands to go to hell, to the unquenchable fire. And if your foot causes you to sin, cut it off; it is better for you to enter life lame than with two feet to be thrown into hell. And if your eye causes you to sin, pluck it out, it is better for you to enter the Kingdom of God with one eye than with two eyes to be thrown into hell.'
Mt. 5:13	'You are the salt of the earth; but if salt has lost its taste, how shall its saltness be restored? It is no longer good for anything except to be thrown out and trodden under foot by men.'
Jn 10:12-13	'He who is a hireling and not a shepherd, whose own the sheep are not, sees the wolf coming and leaves the sheep and flees; and the wolf snatches them and scatters them. He flees because he is a hireling and cares nothing for the sheep.'
Mk 12:34	And when Jesus saw that he answered wisely, he said to him, 'You are not far from the Kingdom of God.' And after that no one dared to ask him any question.
Lk. 13:24-27	And someone said to him, 'Lord, will those who are saved be few?' And he said to them, 'Strive to enter by the narrow door; for many, I tell you, will seek to enter and will not be able. When once the householder has risen up and shut the door, you will begin to stand outside and to knock at the door, saying, "Lord, open to us." He will answer you, "I do not know where you come from." Then you will begin to say, "We ate and drank in your presence, and you taught in our streets." But he will say, "I tell you, I do not know where you come from; depart from me, all you workers of iniquity."'

Mt. 7:20-23 On that day many will say to me, 'Lord, Lord, did we not prophesy in your name, and cast out demons in your name, and do many mighty works in your name?' And then will I declare to them, 'I never knew you; depart from me, you evildoers.'

see also 10. Faith.

14. The Qualities Christ Demands: II

i. Alertness in God's service

Mt. 7:15,16	'Beware of false prophets, who come to you in sheep's clothing but inwardly are ravenous wolves. You will know them by their fruits. Are grapes gathered from thorns, or figs from thistles?'
Mt. 11:13-15	'. . . For all the prophets and the law prophesied until John; and if you are willing to accept it, he is Elijah who is to come. He who has ears to hear, let him hear.'
Mt. 13:23	'. . . As for what was sown on good soil, this is he who hears the word and understands it; he indeed bears fruit, and yields, in one case a hundredfold, in another sixty, and in another thirty.'
Mk 4:21-25	And he said to them, 'Is a lamp brought in to be put under a bushel, or under a bed, and not on a stand? For there is nothing hid, except to be made manifest; nor is anything secret, except to come to light. If any man has ears to ear, let him hear.' And he said to them, 'Take heed what you hear; the measure you give will be the measure you get, and still more will be given you. For to him who has will more be given; and from him who has not, even what he has will be taken away.'
Mt. 10:16	'Behold, I send you out as sheep in the midst of wolves; so be wise as serpents and innocent as doves.'
Lk. 10:23,24	Then turning to the disciples, he said privately, 'Blessed are the eyes which see what you see! For I tell you that many prophets and kings desired to see what you see, and did not see it, and to hear what you hear, and did not hear it.'
Lk. 12:35-38	'Let your loins be girded and your lamps burning, and be like men who are waiting for their master to come home from the marriage feast, so that they may open to him at once when he comes and knocks. Blessed are those servants whom the master finds awake when he comes; truly, I say to you, he will gird himself and have them sit

at table, and he will come and serve them. If he comes in the second watch, or in the third, and finds them so, blessed are those servants.'

Mt. 24:45 'Who then is the faithful and wise servant whom his master has set over his household, to give them their food at the proper time?'

Mt. 16:2,3 He answered them, 'When it is evening, you say, "It will be fair weather; for the sky is red." And in the morning, "It will be stormy today, for the sky is red and threatening." You know how to interpret the appearances of the sky, but you cannot interpret the signs of the times.'

Lk. 16:8 '... The master commended the dishonest steward for his prudence; for the sons of this world are wiser in their own generation than the sons of light.'

Mt. 25:23-30 '... His master said to him, "Well done, good and faithful servant; you have been faithful over a little, I will set you over much; enter into the joy of your master." He also who had received the one talent came forward, saying, "Master, I knew you to be a hard man, reaping where you did not sow, and gathering where you did not winnow; so I was afraid, and I went and hid your talent in the ground. Here you have what is yours." But his master answered him, "You wicked and slothful servant! You knew that I reap where I have not sowed, and gather where I have not winnowed? Then you ought to have invested my money with the bankers, and at my coming I should have received what was my own with interest. So take the talent from him, and give it to him who has the ten talents. For to every one who has will more be given, and he will have abundance; but from him who has not, even what he has will be taken away. And cast the worthless servant into the outer darkness; there men will weep and gnash their teeth."'

Mt. 25:10-12 '... And while they went to buy, the bridegroom came, and those who were ready went in with him to the marriage feast; and the door was shut. Afterward the other maidens came also, saying, "Lord, lord, open to us." But he replied, "Truly, I say to you, I do not know you."'

ii. Peace, courage, and calm

Mt. 14:27-31 — But immediately he spoke to them, saying, 'Take heart, it is I; have no fear.' And Peter answered him, 'Lord, if it is you, bid me come to you on the water.' He said, 'Come'. So Peter got out of the boat and walked on the water and came to Jesus; but when he saw the wind, he was afraid, and beginning to sink he cried out, 'Lord, save me.' Jesus immediately reached out his hand and caught him, saying to him, 'O man of little faith, why did you doubt?'

Mk 8:17 — And being aware of it, Jesus said to them, 'Why do you discuss the fact that you have no bread? Do you not yet perceive or understand? Are your hearts hardened?

Lk. 10:5,6 — . . . Whatever house you enter, first say, 'Peace be to this house.' And if a son of peace is there, your peace shall rest upon him; but if not, it shall return to you.

Lk. 10:41,42 — But the Lord answered her, 'Martha, Martha, you are anxious and troubled about many things; one thing is needful. Mary has chosen the good portion, which shall not be taken away from her.'

Lk. 12:6,7 — '. . . Are not five sparrows sold for two pennies? And not one of them is forgotten before God. Why, even the hairs of your head are all numbered. Fear not; you are of more value than many sparrows.'

Mt. 6:25-34 — 'Therefore I tell you, do not be anxious about your life, what you shall eat or what you shall drink, nor about your body, what you shall put on. Is not life more than food, and the body more than clothing? Look at the birds of the air; they neither sow nor reap nor gather into barns, yet your heavenly Father feeds them. Are you not of more value than they? And which of you by being anxious can add one cubit to his span of life? And why are you anxious about clothing? Consider the lilies of the field, how they grow; they neither toil nor spin, yet I tell you, even Solomon in all his glory was not arrayed like one of these. But if God so clothes the grass of the field, which today is alive and tomorrow thrown into the oven, will he not much more clothe you, O men of little faith? Therefore do not be anxious, saying, "What shall we eat?" or "What shall we drink?" or "What shall we wear?" For the Gentiles seek all these things; and your heavenly Father knows that you need them all. But seek first his kingdom and his righteousness, and all these things shall be yours as well.

'Therefore, do not be anxious about tomorrow, for tomorrow will be anxious for itself. Let the day's own trouble be sufficient for the day.'

Lk. 12:32 'Fear not, little flock, for it is your Father's good pleasure to give you the kingdom.'

Lk. 17:33 '... Whoever seeks to gain his life will lose it, but whoever loses his life will preserve it.'

Lk. 12:24,25 '... Consider the ravens: they neither sow nor reap, they have neither storehouse nor barn, and yet God feeds them. Of how much more value are you than the birds. And which of you by being anxious can add a cubit to his span of life?'

Lk. 21:9 '... And when you hear of wars and tumults, do not be terrified; for this must first take place, but the end will not be at once.'

Lk. 21:16-19 '... You will be delivered up even by parents and brothers and kinsmen and friends, and some of you they will put to death; you will be hated by all for my name's sake. But not a hair of your head will perish. By your endurance you will gain your lives.'

Jn 14:27 '... Peace I leave with you; my peace I give to you; not as the world gives do I give to you. Let not your hearts be troubled, neither let them be afraid.'

Jn 15:7 '... If you abide in me, and my words abide in you, ask whatever you will and it shall be done for you.'

Jn 16:33 '... I have said this to you, that in me you may have peace. In the world you have tribulation; but be of good cheer, I have overcome the world.'

Mt. 26:62 And the high priest stood up and said, 'Have you no answer to make? What is it that these men testify against you?' But Jesus was silent.

Mt. 27:13,14 Then Pilate said to him, 'Do you not hear how many things they testify against you?' But he gave him no

	answer, not even to a single charge; so that the governor wondered greatly.
Lk. 23:9-11	So he questioned him at some length; but he made no answer. The chief priests and the scribes stood by, vehemently accusing him. And Herod with his soldiers treated him with contempt and mocked him; then, arraying him in gorgeous apparel, he sent him back to Pilate.
Jn 19:9	. . . he entered the praetorium again and said to Jesus, 'Where are you from?' But Jesus gave no answer.
Lk. 24:38-40	And he said to them, 'Why are you troubled, and why do questionings rise in your hearts? See my hands and my feet, that it is I myself; handle me, and see; for a spirit has not flesh and bones as you see that I have.' And when he had said this, he showed them his hands and his feet.

See also: 12. Compassion

15. Poverty and self-emptying

i. Poverty

Lk. 1:53	'He has filled the hungry with good things and the rich he has sent empty away.'
Lk. 2:7	'And she gave birth to her first-born son and wrapt him in swaddling cloths, and laid him in a manger, because there was no place for them in the inn.'
Lk. 2:12	'And this will be a sign for you: you will find a babe wrapt in swaddling cloths and lying in a manger.'
Lk. 3:11	And he answered them, 'He that has two coats, let him share with him who has none; and he who has food, let him do likewise.'
Mt. 10:9,10	'Take no gold, nor silver, nor copper in your belts, no bag for your journey, nor two tunics, nor sandals, nor a staff; for the labourer deserves his food.'
Mt. 8:20	'And Jesus said to him, "Foxes have holes, and birds of the air have nests; but the Son of man has nowhere to lay his head." '
Lk. 10:3,4	'Go your way; behold, I send you out as lambs in the midst of wolves. Carry no purse, no bag, no sandals; and salute no-one on the road.'
Lk. 16:13	'No servant can serve two masters; for either he will hate the one and love the other, or he will be devoted to the one and despise the other. You cannot serve God and mammon.'
Mt. 6:26-34	'Look at the birds of the air; they neither sow nor reap nor gather into barns, and yet your heavenly Father feeds them. Are you not of more value than they? And which of you by being anxious can add one cubit to his span of life? And why are you anxious about clothing? Consider the lilies of the field, how they grow; they neither toil nor spin; yet I tell you, even Solomon in all his glory was not arrayed like one of these. But if God so clothes the grass of the field, which today is alive and tomorrow is thrown into the oven, will he not much more clothe you, O men of little faith? Therefore do not be anxious, saying, "What shall we eat?" or, "What shall

we drink?" or, "What shall we wear?" For the Gentiles seek all these things; and your heavenly Father knows that you need them all. But seek first his kingdom and his righteousness and all these things shall be yours as well.

'Therefore do not be anxious about tomorrow, for tomorrow will be anxious for itself. Let the day's own trouble be sufficient for the day.'

Mt. 6:19-21 'Do not lay up for yourselves treasures on earth, where moth and rust consume and where thieves break in and steal, but lay up for yourselves treasures in heaven, where neither moth nor rust consumes and where thieves do not break in and steal. For where your treasure is, there will your heart be also.'

Lk. 12:32-34 'Fear not, little flock, for it is your Father's good pleasure to give you the kingdom. Sell your possessions and give alms; provide yourselves with purses that do not grow old, with a treasure where no thief approaches and no moth destroys. For where your treasure is, there will your heart be also.'

Mk 10:21-27 And Jesus looking upon him loved him, and said to him, 'You lack one thing; go, sell what you have, and give to the poor, and you will have treasure in heaven; and come, follow me.' At that saying his countenance fell, and he went away sorrowful; for he had great possessions.

And Jesus looked around and said to his disciples, 'How hard it will be for those who have riches to enter the kingdom of God.' And the disciples were amazed at his words. But Jesus said to them again, 'Children, how hard it is for those who trust in riches to enter the kingdom of God.' And they were exceedingly astonished and said to him, 'Then who can be saved?' Jesus looked at them and said, 'With men it is impossible, but not with God; for all things are possible with God.'

Mk 10:29,30 'Truly, I say to you, there is no one who has left house or brothers or sisters or mother or father or children or lands, for my sake and for the gospel, who will not receive a hundredfold now in this time, houses and

	brothers and sisters and mothers and children and lands with persecutions, and in the age to come eternal life.'
Lk. 22:35,36	And he said to them, 'When I sent you out with no purse or bag or sandals, did you lack anything?' They said, 'Nothing.' He said to them, 'But now, let him who has a purse take it, and likewise a bag. And let him who has no sword sell his mantle and buy one.'

ii. Littleness

Mt. 16:24-26	Then Jesus told his disciples, 'If any man would come after me, let him deny himself and take up his cross and follow me. For whoever shall save his life will lose it, and whoever loses his life for my sake will find it. For what will it profit a man, if he gains the whole world and forfeits his life?'
Lk. 12:49-53	'I came to cast fire upon earth; and would that it were already kindled. I have a baptism to be baptized with; and how I am constrained until it is accomplished. Do you think that I have come to give peace on earth? No, I tell you, but rather division, for henceforth in one house there will be five divided, three against two and two against three; they will be divided, father against son and son against father, mother against daughter and daughter against her mother, mother-in-law against her daughter-in-law and daughter-in-law against her mother-in-law.'
Lk. 14:10-11	'But when you are invited, go and sit in the lowest place, so that when your host comes he may say to you, 'Friend, go up higher,' then you will be honoured in the presence of all who sit at table with you. For every one who exalts himself will be humbled, and he who humbles himself will be exalted.'
Mt. 10:39	'He who finds his life will lose it, and he who loses his life for my sake will find it.'
Mt. 20:25-28	But Jesus called them to him and said, 'You know that the rulers of the Gentiles lord it over them, and their great men exercise authority over them. It shall not be so among you; but whoever would be great among you must be your servant, and whoever would be first among you must be your slave; even as the Son of man came

not to be served but to serve, and to give his life as a ransom for many.

Jn 12:26 'If anyone serves me, he must follow me; and where I am there shall my servant be also; if any one serves me, the Father will honour him.'

Mt. 23:8-12 But you are not to be called rabbi, for you have one teacher, and you are all brethren. And call no man your father on earth, for you have one Father, who is in heaven. Neither be called masters, for you have one Master, the Christ. He who is greatest among you shall be your servant; whoever exalts himself will be humbled, and whoever humbles himself will be exalted.'

iii. Little ones

Lk. 1:47,48 '. . . and my spirit rejoices in God my Saviour,
for he has regarded the low estate of his handmaiden.'

Lk. 1:51,52 'He has shown strength with his arm,
he has scattered the proud in the imagination of their hearts. . . .'

Lk. 4:17-19 And he stood up to read: and there was given to him the book of the prophet Isaiah. He opened the book and found the place where it was written,
'The Spirit of the Lord is upon me,
because he anointed me to preach the good news to the poor.
He has sent me to proclaim release to the captives
and recovering of sight to the blind,
to set at liberty those who are oppressed,
to proclaim the acceptable year of the Lord.'

Mt. 5:3-12 'Blessed are the poor in spirit, for theirs is the kingdom of heaven.
Blessed are those who mourn, for they shall be comforted.
Blessed are the meek, for they shall inherit the earth.
Blessed are those who hunger and thirst for righteousness, for they shall be satisfied.
Blessed are the merciful, they shall obtain mercy.
Blessed are the pure in heart, for they shall see God.

Blessed are the peacemakers, for they shall be called sons of God.
Blessed are those who are persecuted for righteousness' sake, for theirs is the kingdom of heaven.
Blessed are you when men shall revile you and persecute you and utter all kinds of evil against you falsely on my account.
Rejoice and be glad for your reward is great in heaven, for so men persecuted the prophets who were before you.'

Lk. 6:20-23

And he lifted up his eyes on his disciples, and said:
'Blessed are you poor, for yours is the kingdom of God.
Blessed are you that hunger now, for you shall be satisfied.
Blessed are you that weep now for you shall laugh.
Blessed are you when men hate you, and when they exclude you and revile you, and cast out your name as evil on account of the Son of Man. Rejoice in that day, and leap for joy, for behold your reward is great in heaven; for so their fathers did to the prophets.'

Mk 9:34-36

But they were silent; for on the way they had discussed with one another who was the greatest. And he sat down and called the twelve; and he said to them, 'If any one would be first, he must be last of all and servant of all.' And he took a child, and put him in the midst of them; and taking him in his arms, he said to them, 'Whoever receives one such child in my name receives me; and whoever receives me, receives not me but him who sent me.'

Mt. 18:3-6

And calling to him a child, he put him in the midst of them, and said, 'Truly, I say to you, unless you turn and become like children, you will never enter the Kingdom of heaven. Whoever humbles himself like this child, he is the greatest in the kingdom of heaven. Whoever receives one such child in my name receives me; but whoever causes one of these little ones who believe in me to sin, it would be better for him to have a great millstone fastened round his neck and to be drowned in the depth of the sea.'

Mt. 18:10 'See that you do not despise one of these little ones; for I tell you that in heaven their angels always behold the face of my father who is in heaven . . .'

Mt. 18:14 'So it is not the will of my Father who is in heaven that one of these little ones should perish.'

Mt. 11:25-30 At that time Jesus declared, 'I thank thee Father, Lord of heaven and earth, that thou hast hidden these things from the wise and understanding and revealed them to babes; yea, Father, for such was thy gracious will. All things have been delivered to me by my Father; and no one knows the Son except the Father, and no one knows the Father except the Son and any one to whom the Son chooses to reveal him. Come to me all of you who labour and are heavy laden, and I will give you rest. Take my yoke upon you, and learn from me for I am gentle and lowly in heart, and you will find rest for your souls. For my yoke is easy, and my burden is light.'

Lk. 18:7 'And will not God vindicate his elect, who cry to him day and night? Will he delay long over them?'

Lk. 18:14 'I tell you, this man went down to his house justified rather than the other; for everyone who exalts himself will be humbled; but he who humbles himself will be exalted.'

Mk 10:13-16 And they were bringing children to him, that he might touch them; and the disciples rebuked them. But when Jesus saw it he was indignant, and said to them, 'Let the children come to me, do not hinder them; for to such belongs the kingdom of God. Truly, I say to you, whoever does not receive the kingdom of God like a child shall not enter it'. And he took them in his arms and blessed them, laying his hands upon them.

Mt. 19:30 'But many that are first will be last, and the last first.'

iv. Self-Emptying

Lk. 2:7 And she gave birth to her first-born son and wrapped him in swaddling cloths, and laid him in a manger, because there was no place for them in the inn.

Lk. 2:12 'And this will be a sign for you: you will find a babe wrapped in swaddling cloths and lying in a manger.'

Mt. 2:13 Now when they had departed, behold, an angel of the Lord appeared to Joseph in a dream and said, 'Rise, take the child and his mother, and flee to Egypt, and remain there till I tell you; for Herod is about to search for the child, to destroy him.'

Mt. 8:20 And Jesus said to him, 'Foxes have holes, and birds of the air have nests; but the Son of man has nowhere to lay his head.'

Mt. 10:25 'It is enough for the disciple to be like his teacher, and the servant like his master. If they have called the master of the house Beelzebul, how much more will they malign those of his household.'

Mt. 21:5 'Tell the daughter of Zion,
Behold, your King is coming to you,
humble, and mounted on an ass,
and on a colt, the foal of an ass.'

Jn 13:12,17 When he had washed their feet, and taken his garments, and resumed his place, he said to them, 'Do you know what I have done to you? You call me Teacher and Lord; and you are right, for so I am. If I then, your Lord and Teacher, have washed your feet, you also ought to wash one another's feet. For I have given you an example, that you also should do as I have done to you. Truly, truly, I say to you, a servant is not greater than his master; nor is he who is sent greater than he who sent him. If you know these things, blessed are you if you do them.'

Lk. 22:37 'For I tell you that this scripture must be fulfilled in me, "And he was reckoned with transgressors"; for what is written about me has its fulfilment.'

Jn 15:20 'Remember the word that I said to you, "A servant is not greater than his master." If they persecuted me, they will persecute you; if they kept my word, they will keep your also.'

Mk 14:33,36 And he took with him Peter and James and John, and began to be greatly distressed and troubled. And he said to them, 'My soul is very sorrowful, even to death; remain here and watch.' And going a little further, he fell on the ground and prayed that, if it were possible, the hour might pass from him. And he said, 'Abba, Father, all things are possible to thee; remove this cup from me; yet not what I will, but what thou wilt.'

Mt. 27:28,30 And they stripped him and put a scarlet robe upon him, and plaiting a crown of thorns they put it on his head, and put a reed in his right hand. And kneeling before him they mocked him saying, 'Hail, King of the Jews.' And they spat upon him and took the reed and struck him on the head.

Mk 15:26,30 And the inscription of the charge against him, read, 'The King of the Jews'. And with him they crucified two robbers, one on his right and one on his left. And those who passed by derided him, wagging their heads, and saying, 'Aha! You who would destroy the temple and build it in three days, save yourself, and come down from the cross.'

Mk 15:34 And at the ninth hour Jesus cried with a loud voice, 'Eloi, Eloi, lama sabachthani?' which means, 'My God, my God, why hast thou forsaken me?'

v. Riches

Lk. 1:53 He has filled the hungry with good things, and the rich he has sent empty away.

Lk. 6:24,25 'But woe to you that are rich, for you have received your consolation.
Woe to you that are full now, for you shall hunger.
Woe to you that laugh now, for you shall mourn and weep.'

Lk. 12:13-15 One of the multitude said to him, 'Teacher, bid my brother divide the inheritance with me.' But he said to him. 'Man, who made me a judge or divider over you'? And he said to them, 'Take heed, and beware of all covetousness; for a man's life does not consist in the abundance of his possessions.'

Lk. 12:20-21 'But God said to him, "Fool! This night your soul is required of you; and the things you have prepared, whose will they be?" So is he who lays up treasure for himself, and is not rich toward God.'

Mt. 6:25 'Therefore I tell you, do not be anxious about your life, what you shall eat or what you shall drink, nor about your body, what you shall put on. Is not life more than food, and the body more than the clothing?'

Lk. 16:11,15 'If then you have not been faithful in the unrighteous mammon, who will entrust to you the true riches? And if you have not been faithful in that which is another's, who will give you that which is your own? No servant can serve two masters; for either he will hate the one and love the other, or he will be devoted to the one and despise the other. You cannot serve God and mammon.'

The Pharisees, who were lovers of money, heard all this, and they scoffed at him. But he said to them, 'You are those who justify yourselves before men, but God knows your hearts; for what is exalted among men is an abomination in the sight of God.'

Lk. 16:25 But Abraham said, 'Son, remember that you in your lifetime received your good things, and Lazarus in like manner evil things, but now he is comforted here, and you are in anguish.'

Mk 10:21,27 And he said to him, 'Teacher, all these I have observed from my youth.' And Jesus looking upon him loved him, and said to him, 'You lack one thing; go, sell what you have, and give to the poor, and you will have treasure in heaven; and come, follow me.' At that saying his countenance fell, and he went away sorrowful; for he had great possessions.

And Jesus looked around and said to his disciples, 'How hard it will be for those who have riches to enter the kingdom of God.' And the disciples were amazed at his words. But Jesus said to them again, 'Children, how hard it is for those who trust in riches to enter the kingdom of God. It is easier for a camel to go through the eye of a needle than for a rich man to enter the kingdom of God.' And they were exceedingly astonished, and said to him, 'Then who can be saved?' Jesus looked at them and said, 'With man it is impossible, but not with God; for all things are possible with God.'

vi. Pride

Lk. 4:5,6 — And the devil took him up, and showed him all the kingdoms of the world in a moment of time, and said to him, 'To you will I give all this authority and their glory; for it has been delivered to me, and I give it to whom I will.'

Lk. 6:24-26 — 'But woe to you that are rich, for you have received your consolation.
Woe to you that are full now, for you shall hunger.
Woe to you that laugh now, for you shall mourn and weep.
Woe to you, when all men speak well of you, for so their fathers did to the false prophets.'

Mt. 6:1-5 — 'Beware of practising your piety before men in order to be seen by them; for then you will have no reward from your Father who is in heaven. Thus, when you give alms, sound no trumpet before you, as the hypocrites do in the synagogues and in the streets, that they may be praised by man. Truly, I say to you, they have their reward. And when you give alms, do not let your left hand know what your right hand is doing, so that your alms may be in secret; and your Father who sees in secret will reward you. And when you pray, you must not be like the hypocrites; for they love to stand and pray in the synagogues and at the street corners, that they may be seen by men. Truly, I say to you, they have their reward.'

Mt. 6:16,17 — 'And when you fast, do not look dismal, like the hypocrites, for they disfigure their faces that their fasting may be seen by men. Truly, I say to you, they have their reward. But when you fast, anoint your head and wash your face.'

Lk. 16:15 — But he said to them, 'You are those who justify yourselves before men, but God knows your hearts; for what is exalted among men is an abomination in the sight of God.'

Lk. 18:4 'I tell you, this man went down to his house justified rather than the other; for everyone who exalts himself will be humbled, but he who humbles himself will be exalted.'

Mt. 20:21-24 And he said to her, 'What do you want?' She said to him, 'Command that these two sons of mine may sit, one at your right hand and one at your left, in your kingdom.' But Jesus answered, 'You do not know what you are asking. Are you able to drink the cup that I am to drink?' They said to him, 'We are able.' He said to them, 'You will drink my cup, but to sit at my right hand and at my left is not mine to grant, but it is for those for whom it has been prepared by my Father.' And when the ten heard it, they were indignant at the two brothers.

Mt. 23:5-7 'They do all their deeds to be seen by men; for they make their phylacteries broad and their fringes long, and they love the place of honour at feasts and the best seats in the synagogues, and salutations in the market places, and being called rabbi by men.'

Lk. 22:24,27 A dispute also arose among them, which of them was to be regarded as the greatest. And he said to them,' The kings of the Gentiles exercise lordship over them; and those in authority over them are called benefactors. But not so with you – rather let the greatest among you become as the youngest, and the leader as one who serves. For which is the greater, one who sits at table, or one who serves? Is it not the one who sits at table? But I am among you as one who serves.'

Jn 13:37,38 Peter said to him, 'Lord, why cannot I follow you now? I will lay down my life for you.' Jesus answered, 'Will you lay down your life for me? Truly, truly, I say to you, the cock will not crow, till you have denied me three times.'

See also: 1.vi. Austerity.

16. Chastity

i. Chastity

Mt. 19:10-12 The disciples said to him, 'If such is the case of a man with his wife, it is not expedient to marry.' But he said to them, 'Not all men can receive this precept, but only those to whom it is given. For there are eunuchs who have been so from birth, and there are eunuchs who have been made eunuchs by men, and there are eunuchs who have made themselves eunuchs for the kingdom of heaven. He who is able to receive it, let him receive it.'

Lk. 20:34-36 And Jesus said to them, 'The sons of this age marry and are given in marriage; but those who are accounted worthy to attain to that age and to the resurrection from the dead neither marry nor are given in marriage, for they cannot die any more, because they are equal to angels and are sons of God, being sons of the resurrection.'

ii. Chastity's Opposites

Mk 6:18 For John said to Herod, 'It is not lawful for you to have your brother's wife.'

Jn 4:17,18 The woman answered him, 'I have no husband.' Jesus said to her, 'You are right in saying, "I have no husband", for you have had five husbands, and he whom you now have is not your husband; this you said truly.'

Mt. 5:27-30 'You have heard that it was said, "You shall not commit adultery." But I say to you that everyone who looks at a woman lustfully has already committed adultery with her in his heart. If your right eye causes you to sin, pluck it out and throw it away; it is better that you lose one of your members than that your whole body be thrown into hell. And if your right hand causes you to sin, cut it off and throw it away; it is better that you lose one of your members than that your whole body go into hell.'

Lk. 16:18 'Everyone who divorces his wife and marries another commits adultery, and he who marries a woman divorced from her husband commits adultery.

Mt. 5:31-32 'It was also said "Whoever divorces his wife, let him give her a certificate of divorce." But I say to you that every one who divorces his wife, except on the ground of unchastity, makes her an adultress; and whoever marries a divorced woman commits adultery.'

Mk 7:21-23 'For from within, out of the heart of man, come evil thoughts, fornication, theft, murder, adultery, coveting, wickedness, deceit, licentiousness, envy, slander, pride, foolishness. All these evil things come from within, and they defile a man.'

Mk 10:4-12 They said, 'Moses allowed a man to write a certificate of divorce, and to put her away.' But Jesus said to them, 'For your hardness of heart he wrote you this commandment. But from the beginning of creation "God made them male and female." "For this reason a man shall leave his father and mother and be joined to his wife and the two shall become one." So they are no longer two but one, What therefore God has joined together, let not man put asunder.

'And in the house the Disciples asked him again about this matter. And he said to them, 'Whoever divorces his wife and marries another, commits adultery against her; and if she divorces her husband and marries another, she commits adultery.'

Mt. 19:9 'And I say to you; whoever divorces his wife, except for unchastity, and marries another, commits adultery; and he who marries a divorced woman commits adultery.'

Mk 10:19 'You know the commandments: "Do not kill, Do not commit adultery, Do not steal, Do not bear false witness, Do not defraud, Honour your father and mother."'

17. Obedience

i. Obedience to the Father

Lk. 1:30	And the angel said to her. 'Do not be afraid Mary, for you have found favour with God.'
Lk. 1:38	And Mary said, 'Behold, I am the handmaid of the Lord; let it be done to me according to your word.'
Lk. 2:29	And he said to them, 'How is it that you sought me? Did you not know that I must be in my Father's house?'
Mt. 3:15	But Jesus answered him, 'Let it be so now, for thus it is fitting for us to fulfill all righteousness.'
Mt. 4:4	But he answered, 'It is written, "Man shall not live by bread alone, but by every word that proceeds from the mouth of God." '
Mt. 12:48-50	But he replied to the man who told him, 'Who is my mother, and who are my brethren?' And stretching out his hand toward his disciples, he said, 'Here are my mother and my brethren! For whoever does the will of my Father in heaven is my brother, and sister, and mother.'
Mk 7:21	'For from within, out of the heart of man, come evil thoughts, fornication, theft, murder, adultery . . . .'
Jn 9:31	'We know that God does not listen to sinners, but if anyone is a worshipper of God and does his will, God listens to him.'
Lk. 11:27,28	And as he said this, a woman in the crowd raised her voice and said to him, 'Blessed is the womb that bore you, and the breasts that you sucked.' But he said, 'Blessed rather are those who hear the word of God and keep it.'
Mk 12:29-31	'Which commandment is the first of all?' Jesus answered, 'The first is, "Hear, O Israel; The Lord our God, the Lord is one; and you shall love the Lord your God with all your heart and with all your soul, and with all your mind, and with all your strength." The second is this, "You shall love your neighbour as yourself." There is no other commandment greater than these.'

Lk. 17:9,10	'Does he thank the servant because he did what was commanded? So you also, when you have done all that is commanded you say, "We are unworthy servants; we have only done what was our duty." '
Jn 14:31	'. . . but I do as the Father has commanded me, so that the world may know that I love the Father.'

ii. Obedience to Christ

Jn 2:5	His mother said to the servants, 'Do whatever he tells you.'
Lk. 5:5	And Simon answered, 'Master, we toiled all night and took nothing! But at your word I will let down the nets.'
Lk. 6:47,48	'Every one who comes to me and hears my words and does them, I will show you what he is like: he is like a man building a house, who dug deep, and laid the foundation upon rock; and when a flood arose the stream broke against that house, and could not shake it, because it had been well built.'
Mt. 8:8,10	But the centurion answered him, 'Lord, I am not worthy to have you come under my roof; but only say the word, and my servant will be healed. For I am a man under authority, with soldiers under me; and I say to one, "Go," and he goes, and to another, "Come," and he comes, and to my slave, "Do this," and he does it.' When Jesus heard him, he marvelled, and said to those who followed him, 'Truly, I say to you, not even in Israel have I found such faith.'
Mt. 14:28,29	And Peter answered him, 'Lord, if it is you, bid me come to you on the water,' He said, 'Come.' So Peter got out of the boat and walked on the water and came to Jesus.
Mk 8:38	'For whoever is ashamed of me and of my words in this adulterous and sinful generation, of him will the Son of man also be ashamed.'
Jn 8:31,32	Jesus then said to the Jews who had believed in him, 'If you continue in my word, you are truly my disciples, and you will know the truth, and the truth will make you free.'

Jn 8:51 'Truly, truly, I say to you, If any one keeps my word, he will never see death.'

Lk. 12:36,37 '... and be like men who are waiting for their master to come home from the marriage feast, so that they may open to him at once when he comes and knocks. Blessed are those servants whom the master finds awake when he comes; truly, I say to you, he will gird himself and have them sit at table, and he will serve them.'

Lk. 12:43,44 'Blessed is that servant whom his master when he comes will find so doing. Truly, I tell you, he will set him over all his possessions.'

Jn 14:15,16 'If you love me, you will keep my commandments. And I will pray the Father, and he will give you another Counsellor, to be with you for ever.'

Jn 14:21-24 'He who has my commandments and keeps them, he it is who loves me; and he who loves me will be loved by my Father and I will love him.' Judas (not Iscariot) said to him, 'Lord, how is it that you will manifest yourself to us, and not to the world?' Jesus answered him, 'If a man loves me, he will keep my word, and my Father will love him, and we will come to him and make our home with him. He who does not love me does not keep my words; and the word which you hear is not mine but the Father's who sent me.'

Jn 15:12,14 'This is my commandment, that you love one another as I have loved you. Greater love has no man than this, that a man lay down his life for his friends. You are my friends if you do what I command you.'

iii. Obedience to religious authority

Lk. 1:6 And they were both righteous before God, walking in all the commandments and ordinances of the Lord blameless.

Lk. 2:22-24 And when the time came for their purification according to the law of Moses, they brought him up to Jerusalem to present him to the Lord (as it is written in the law of the Lord, 'Every male that opens the womb shall be called holy to the Lord.') and to offer a sacrifice according to what is said in the law of the Lord, 'a pair of turtledoves or two young pigeons.'

Lk. 2:39-41 And when they had performed everything according to the law of the Lord, they returned into Galilee, to their own city Nazareth. And the child grew and became strong, filled with wisdom; and the favour of God was upon him.

Now his parents went to Jerusalem every year at the feast of the Passover.

Mt. 8:4 And Jesus said to him, 'See that you say nothing to any one; but go, show yourself to the priest, and offer the gift that Moses commanded, for a proof to the people.'

Mt. 5:17-20 'Think not that I have come to abolish the law and the prophets; I have not come to abolish them but to fulfil them. For truly I say to you, till heaven and earth pass away, not an iota, not a dot, will pass from the law until all is accomplished. Whoever then relaxes one of the least of these commandments and teaches men so, shall be called least in the kingdom of heaven; but he who does them and teaches them shall be called great in the kingdom of heaven.'

Mt. 17:23 'The Son of man is to be delivered into the hands of men, and they will kill him, and he will be raised on the third day.' And they were greatly distressed.

Mt. 23:2,3 'The scribes and the Pharisees sit on Moses' seat; so practise and observe whatever they tell you, but not what they do; for they preach, but do not practise.'

Mt. 26:63,64 And the high priest said to him, 'I adjure you by the living God, tell us if you are the Christ, the Son of God.' Jesus said to him, 'You have said so. But I tell you hereafter you will see the Son of Man seated at the right hand of Power, and coming on the clouds of heaven.'

iv. Obedience to human authority

Lk. 2:1,4,5 In those days a decree went out from Caesar Augustus that all the world should be enrolled. And Joseph also went up from Galilee, from the city of Nazareth, to Judea, to the city of David, to be enrolled with Mary, his betrothed, who was with child.

Lk. 2:50-52 And they did not understand the saying which he spoke to them. And he went down with them and came to Nazareth, and was obedient to them; and his mother kept all these things in her heart.

And Jesus increased in wisdom and in stature, and in favour with God and man.

Mt. 22:20,21 And Jesus said to them, 'Whose likeness and inscription is this?' They said, 'Caesar's.' Then he said to them, 'Render therefore to Caesar the things that are Caesar's, and to God the things that are God's.'

Jn 19:11 Jesus answered Pilate, 'You would have no power over me unless it had been given you from above; therefore he who delivered me to you has the greater sin.'

v. Obedience to men who have Christ's authority

Mt. 16:18-19 'And I tell you, you are Peter, and on this rock I will build my church, and the powers of death shall not prevail against it. I will give you the keys of the kingdom of heaven and whatever you bind on earth shall be bound in heaven, and whatever you loose on earth shall be loosed in heaven.'

Mt. 10:14 'And if any one will not receive you or listen to your words, shake off the dust from your feet as you leave that house or town.'

Mt. 18:16-18 'But if he does not listen, take one or two others along with you, that every word may be confirmed by the evidence of two or three witnesses. If he refuses to listen to them, tell it to the church; and if he refuses to listen even to the church, let him be to you as a Gentile and a tax collector. Truly, I say to you, whatever you bind on earth shall be bound in heaven, and whatever you loose on earth shall be loosed in heaven.'

Lk. 10:16 'He who hears you hears me, and he who rejects you rejects me, and he who rejects me rejects him who sent me.'

Mt. 28:18-20 And Jesus came and said to them, 'All authority in heaven and on earth has been given to me. Go therefore and make disciples of all nations, baptizing them in the name of the Father and of the Son and of the Holy Spirit, teaching them to observe all that I have commanded you; and lo, I am with you always, to the close of the age.'

vi. The value and rewards of obedience

Lk. 2:39,40	And when they had performed everything according to the law of the Lord, they returned into Galilee, to their own city, Nazareth. And the child grew and became strong, filled with wisdom; and the favour of God was upon him.
Lk. 2:51,52	And he went down with them and came to Nazareth, and was obedient to them; and his mother kept all these things in her heart. And Jesus increased in wisdom and stature, and in favour with God and man.
Lk. 5:8-11	But when Simon Peter saw it, he fell down at Jesus' knees, saying, 'Depart from me, for I am a sinful man, O Lord.' For he was astonished, and all that were with him, at the catch of fish which they had taken; and so also were James and John, sons of Zebedee, who were partners with Simon. And Jesus said to Simon, 'Do not be afraid; henceforth you will be catching men.' And when they had brought their boats to land, they left everything and followed him.
Mt. 7:21	'Not every one who says to me, "Lord, Lord," shall enter the kingdom of heaven, but he who does the will of my Father who is in heaven.'
Lk. 6:47,48	'Everyone who comes to me and hears my words and does them, I will show you what he is like: he is like a man building a house, who dug deep, and laid the foundation upon a rock; and when the flood arose, the stream broke against that house, and could not shake it, because it had been well built.'
Jn 7:16,17	Jesus answered them, 'My teaching is not mine, but his who sent me; if any man's will is to do his will, he shall know whether the teaching is from God or whether I am speaking on my own authority.'
Jn 8:31,32	Jesus then said to the Jews who had believed in him, 'If you continue in my word, you are truly my disciples, and

you will know the truth and the truth will make you free.

Jn 8:51 'Truly, truly, I say to you, if any one keeps my word, he will never see death.'

Lk. 11:27,28 As he said this, a woman in the crowd raised her voice and said to him, 'Blessed is the womb that bore you, and the breasts that you sucked.' But he said, 'Blessed rather are those who hear the word of God and keep it.'

Lk. 12:43,44 'Blessed is that servant whom his master when he comes will find so doing. Truly, I tell you, he will set him over all his possessions.'

Mt. 5:18,19 'For truly, I say to you, till heaven and earth pass away, not an iota, not a dot, will pass from the law until all is accomplished. Whoever then relaxes one of the least of these commandments and teaches man so, shall be called least in the kingdom of heaven; but he who does them and teaches them shall be called great in the kingdom of heaven.'

Lk. 16:29 But Abraham said, 'They have Moses and the prophets; let them hear them.'

Mk 10:20,21 And he said to him, 'Teacher, all these I have observed from my youth.' And Jesus looking upon him, loved him, and said to him, 'You lack one thing; go, sell what you have, and give to the poor, and you will have treasure in heaven; and come, follow me.'

Mk 10:29,30 Jesus said; 'Truly, I say to you, there is no one who has left house or brothers or sisters or mother or father or children or lands, for my sake and for the gospel, who will not receive a hundredfold now in this time, houses and brothers and sisters and mothers and children and lands, with persecutions, and in the age to come eternal life.'

Jn 12:26 'If any one serves me, he must follow me: and where I am, there shall my servant be also; if any one serves me, the Father will honour him.'

Mt. 21:28-31 'What do you think? A man had two sons; and he went to the first and said, "Son, go and work in the vineyard today." And he answered, "I will not"; but afterward he repented and went. And he went to the second and said the same; and he answered, "I go, sir," but did not go. Which of the two did the will of the father?' They said, 'The first.' Jesus said to them, 'Truly, I say to you, the tax collectors and the harlots go into the kingdom of God before you.'

Jn 14:15,16 'If you love me, you will keep my commandments. And I will pray the Father, and he will give you another Counsellor, to be with you for ever.'

Jn 14:21-24 'He who has my commandments and keeps them, he it is who loves me; and he who loves me will be loved by my Father, and I will love him and manifest myself to him.' Judas (not Iscariot) said to him, 'Lord, how is it that you will manifest yourself to us, and not to the world?' Jesus answered him, 'If a man loves me, he will keep my word, and my Father will love him, and we will come to him and make our home with him. He who does not love me does not keep my words; and the word which you hear is not mine but the father's who sent me.'

Jn 15:12-14 'This is my commandment, that you love one another as I have loved you. Greater love has no man than this, that a man lay down his life for his friends. You are my friends if you do what I command you.'

vii. The urgency of obedience

Mk 8:38 'For whosoever is ashamed of me and of my words in this adulterous and sinful generation, of him will the Son of man also be ashamed.'

Mk 9:42-48 'Whosoever causes one of these little ones who believe in me to sin, it would be better for him that a great millstone were hung around his neck, and he were thrown into the sea. And if your hand causes you to sin, cut it off; it is better for you to enter life maimed than with two hands to go to hell, to the unquenchable fire. And if your foot causes you to sin, cut it off; it is better for you to enter life lame than with two feet to be thrown into hell. And if your eye causes you to sin, pluck it out; it is better for you to enter the kingdom of God with one eye, than with two eyes to be thrown into hell, where their worm does not die, and the fire is not quenched.'

Lk. 9:59-62 — To another he said, 'Follow me'. But he said, 'Lord, let me first go and bury my father.' But he said to him, 'Leave the dead to bury their own dead; but as for you, go and proclaim the kingdom of God.' Another said, 'I will follow you Lord; but let me first say farewell to those at my home.' Jesus said to him, 'No one who puts his hand to the plough and looks back is fit for the kingdom of God.'

Lk. 12:47-48 — 'And that servant who knew his master's will, but did not make ready or act according to his will, shall receive a severe beating. But he who did not know, and did what deserved a beating, shall receive a light beating. Every one to whom much is given, of him will much be required; and of him to whom men commit much they will demand the more.'

Lk. 17:32-33 — 'Remember Lot's wife. Whoever seeks to gain his life will lose it, but whoever loses his life will preserve it.'

viii. Disobedience

Lk. 6:49 — 'But he who hears, and does not do them is like a man who built a house on the ground without a foundation; against which the stream broke, and immediately it fell, and the ruin of that house was great.'

Mt. 14:30 — But when he saw the wind, he was afraid and beginning to sink he cried out, 'Lord, save me.'

Jn 8:37 — 'I know that you are descendants of Abraham; yet you seek to kill me, because my words find no place in you.'

Lk. 10:10-12 — 'But whenever you enter a town and they do not receive you, go into its streets and say, "Even the dust of your town that clings to our feet, we wipe off against you; nevertheless know this, that the kingdom of God has come near." I tell you, it shall be more tolerable on that day for Sodom than for that town.'

Lk. 12:47,48 — 'And that servant who knew his master's will, but did not make ready or act according to his will shall receive a severe beating. But he who did not know, and did what deserved a beating, shall receive a light beating. Every-one to whom much is given, of him will much be required; and of him to whom men commit much they will demand the more.'

See also: 4.v. Jesus does the Father's will
10. Faith

18. The Failures that Provoke Christ

i. Culpable blindness

Lk. 3:8,9 'Bear fruits that befit repentance, and do not begin to say to yourselves, "We have Abraham as our father;" for I tell you, God is able from these stones to raise up children to Abraham. Even now the axe is laid to the root of the trees, every tree therefore that does not bear good fruit is cut down and thrown into the fire.'

Lk. 5:21,22 And the scribes and the Pharisees began to question, saying 'Who is this that speaks blasphemies? Who can forgive sins but God only?' When Jesus perceived their questionings, he answered them, 'Why do you question in your hearts?'

Mt. 9:11-13 And when the Pharisees saw this, they said to his disciples, 'Why does your teacher eat with tax collectors and sinners?' But when he heard it, he said, 'Those who are well have no need of a physician but those who are sick. Go and learn what this means, "I desire mercy and not sacrifice." For I came not to call the righteous but sinners.'

Lk. 6:9 And Jesus said to them, 'I ask you, is it lawful on the sabbath to do good or to do harm, to save life or to destroy it?'

Mt. 11:16-19 'But to what shall I compare this generation? it is like children sitting in the market place and calling to their playmates, "We piped to you and you did not dance; We wailed and you did not mourn." For John came neither eating nor drinking, and they say, "He has a demon;" the Son of man came eating and drinking, and they say, "Behold a glutton and a drunkard, a friend of tax collectors and sinners." Yet wisdom is justified by her deeds.'

Mt. 13:14,15 'With them indeed is fulfilled the prophecy of Isaiah which says,
"You shall indeed hear but never understand,
and you shall indeed see but never perceive.
For this people's heart has grown dull,
and their ears are heavy of hearing,

and their eyes they have closed, lest they should perceive with their eyes,
and hear with their ears,
and understand with their heart,
and turn for me to heal them."'

Mt. 15:14 'Let them alone. They are blind guides. And if a blind man leads a blind man, both will fall into a pit.'

Mt. 16:4 'An evil and adulterous generation seeks for a sign but no sign shall be given it except the sign of Jonah'. So he left them and departed.

Mt. 18:15-17 'If your brother sins against you, go and tell him his fault, between you and him alone. If he listens to you, you have gained your brother. But if he does not listen to you, take one or two others along with you, that every word may be confirmed by the evidence of two or three witnesses. If he refuses to listen to them, tell it to the church, and if he refuses to listen even to the church, let him be to you as a gentile and a tax collector.'

Mt. 11:20 Then he began to upbraid the cities where most of his mighty works had been done, because they did not repent.

Lk. 9:54-56 And when his disciples James and John saw it, they said, 'Lord, do you want us to bid fire come down from heaven and consume them?' But he turned and rebuked them. And they went on to another village.

Jn 7:23,24 'If on the sabbath a man receives circumcision, so that the law of Moses may not be broken, are you angry with me because on the sabbath I made a man's whole body well? Do not judge by appearances, but judge with right judgment.'

Jn 8:19 They said to him therefore, 'Where is your Father?' Jesus answered, 'You know neither me nor my Father; if you knew me, you would know my Father also.'

Jn 8:37,38 'I know that you are descendants of Abraham; yet you seek to kill me, because my word finds no place in you. I speak of what I have seen with my Father, and you do what you have heard from your father.'

Jn 8:43-47 'Why do you not understand what I say? It is because you cannot bear to hear my word. You are of your father the devil, and your will is to do your father's desires. He was a murderer from the beginning, and has nothing to do with the truth, because there is no truth in him. When he lies, he speaks according to his own nature, for he is a liar and the father of lies. But, because I tell you the truth, you do not believe me. Which of you convicts me of sin? If I tell the truth, why do you not believe me? He who is of God hears the words of God; the reason why you do not hear them is that you are not of God.'

Jn 9:39-41 Jesus said, 'For judgment I came into this world, that those who do not see may see, and that those who see may become blind.' Some of the Pharisees near him heard this, and they said to him, 'Are we also blind?' Jesus said to them, 'If you were blind, you would have no guilt; but now that you say, 'We see', your guilt remains.'

Mk 3:28-30 'Truly, I say to you, all sins will be forgiven the sons of men, and whatever blasphemies they utter; but whoever blasphemes against the Holy Spirit never has forgiveness, but is guilty of an eternal sin' – for they had said, 'He has an unclean spirit.'

Mt. 12:38-42 Then some of the scribes and Pharisees said to him, 'Teacher, we wish to see a sign from you.' But he answered them, 'An evil and adulterous generation seeks for a sign; but no sign shall be given to it except the sign of the prophet Jonah. For as Jonah was three days and three nights in the belly of the whale, so will the Son of man be three days and three nights in the heart of the earth.'

Mt. 10:24,25 'A disciple is not above his teacher, nor a servant above his master; it is enough for the disciple to be like his teacher, and the servant like his master. If they have called the master of the house Beelzebul, how much more will they malign those of his household.'

Mt. 6:23 '. . . but if your eye is not sound, your whole body will be full of darkness. If then the light in you is darkness, how great is the darkness.'

Mt. 10:10-16 'But whenever you enter a town and they do not receive you, go into its streets and say, "Even the dust of your town that clings to our feet, we wipe off against you; nevertheless know this, that the kingdom of God has come near." I tell you, it shall be more tolerable on that day for Sodom than for that town.

'Woe to you, Chorazin! woe to you, Bethsaida! for if the mighty works done in you had been done in Tyre and Sidon, they would have repented long ago, sitting in sackcloth and ashes. But it shall be more tolerable in the judgment for Tyre and Sidon than for you. And you, Capernaum, will you be exalted to heaven? You shall be brought down to Hades.

'He who hears you hears me, and he who rejects you rejects me, and he who rejects me rejects him who sent me.'

Lk. 11:32 'The men of Nineveh will arise at the judgment with this generation and condemn it; for they repented at the preaching of Jonah, and behold, something greater than Jonah is here.

Lk. 11:40-42 'You fools! Did not he who made the outside make the inside also? But give for alms those things which are within; and behold, everything is clean for you.

'But woe to you Pharisees! for you tithe mint and rue and every herb, and neglect justice and the love of God; these you ought to have done, without neglecting the others.'

Mt. 23:34 'Therefore I send you prophets and wise men and scribes, some of whom you will kill and crucify, and some you will scourge in your synagogues and persecute from town to town.'

Lk. 13:15,16 Then the Lord answered him, 'You hypocrites! Does not each of you on the sabbath untie his ox or his ass from the manger, and lead it away to water it? And ought not this woman, a daughter of Abraham whom Satan bound for eighteen years, be loosed from this bond on the sabbath day?'

Lk. 13:32,33 And he said to them, 'Go and tell that fox, "Behold, I cast out demons and perform cures today and tomorrow, and the third day I finish my course. Nevertheless I must go on my way today and tomorrow and the day following; for it cannot be that a prophet should perish away from Jerusalem."'

Lk. 15:5 — And he said to them, 'Which of you, having an ass or an ox that has fallen into a well, will not immediately pull him out on a sabbath day?'

Lk. 19:41,42 — And when he drew near and saw the city he wept over it, saying, 'Would that even today you knew the things that make for peace! But now they are hid from your eyes.'

Mt. 21:28-32 — 'What do you think? A man had two sons; and he went to the first and said, "Son go and work in the vineyard today." And he answered, "I will not;" but afterwards he repented and went. And he went to the second and said the same; and he answered, "I go, sir," but did not go. Which of the two did the will of his father?' They said, 'The first.' Jesus said to them, 'Truly, I say to you, the tax collectors and the harlots go into the kingdom of God before you. For John came to you in the way of righteousness, and you did not believe him, but the tax collectors and the harlots believed him; and even when you saw it, you did not afterward repent and believe him.'

Mt. 23:13-32 — 'But woe to you, scribes and Pharisees, hypocrites! because you shut the kingdom of heaven against men; for you neither enter yourself, nor allow those who would enter to go in. Woe to you, scribes and Pharisees, hypocrites! for you traverse sea and land to make a single proselyte, and when he becomes a proselyte, you make him twice as much a child of hell as yourself.

'Woe to you, blind guides, who say, "If any one swears by the temple, it is nothing; but if any one swears by the gold of the temple, he is bound by his oath." You blind fools! For which is greater, the gold, or the temple that has made the gold sacred? And you say, "If any one swears by the altar, it is nothing; but if any one swears by the gift that is on the altar, he is bound by his oath." You blind men! For which is greater, the gift or the altar that makes the gift sacred? So he who swears by the altar, swears by it and by everything on it; and he who swears by the temple, swears by it and by him who dwells in it, and he who swears by heaven, swears by the throne of God and by Him who sits upon it.

'Woe to you, scribes and Pharisees, hypocrites! for you tithe mint and dill and cummin, and have neglected the weightier matters of the law, justice and mercy and faith; these you ought to have done without neglecting the others. You blind guides, straining out a gnat and swallowing a camel!

'Woe to you, scribes, and Pharisees, hypocrites! for you are like white-washed tombs, which outwardly appear beautiful, but within they are full of dead men's bones and all uncleanness. So you also outwardly appear righteous to men, but within you are full of hypocrisy and iniquity.

'Woe to you, scribes and Pharisees, hypocrites! for you build the tombs of the prophets and adorn the monuments of the righteous saying, "If we had lived in the days of our fathers, we would not have taken part with them in shedding the blood of the prophets." Thus you witness against yourselves, that you are sons of those who murdered the prophets. Fill up, then, the measure of your fathers.'

Mt. 23:33-36

'You serpents, you brood of vipers, how are you to escape being sentenced to hell? Therefore I send you prophets and wise men and scribes, some of whom you will kill and crucify, and some you will scourge in your synagogues and persecute from town to town, that upon you may come all the righteous blood shed on earth, from the blood of innocent Abel to the blood of Zechariah the son of Barachiah, whom you murdered between the sanctuary and the altar. Truly, I say to you, all this will come upon this generation.'

Jn 12:37-41

Though he had done so many signs before them, yet they did not believe in him; it was that the word spoken by the prophet Isaiah might be fulfilled: 'Lord, who has believed our report, and to whom has the arm of the Lord been revealed?' Therefore they could not believe. For Isaiah again said: 'He has blinded their eyes and hardened their heart, lest they should see with their eyes and perceive with their heart, and turn for me to heal them.' Isaiah said this because he saw his glory and spoke of him.

Mt. 25:44-46 'Then they also will answer, "Lord, when did we see thee hungry or thirsty or a stranger or naked or sick or in prison, and did not minister to thee?" Then he will answer them, "Truly, I say to you, as you did it not to one of the least of these, you did it not to me." And they will go away into eternal punishment, but the righteous into eternal life.'

Jn 15:22 'If I had not come and spoken to them, they would not have sin; but now they have no excuse for their sin.'

Jn 15:24 'If I had not done among them the works which no one else did, they would not have sin; but now they have seen and hated both me and my Father.'

Mt. 27:4,5 [Judas said] 'I have sinned in betraying innocent blood.' They said, 'What is that to us? See to it yourself.' And throwing down the pieces of silver in the temple, he departed; and he went and hanged himself.

ii. Sham, hypocrisy, pretence

Mt. 6:1-6 'Beware of practising your piety before man in order to be seen by them, for then you will have no reward from your Father who is in heaven. Thus, when you give alms, sound no trumpet before you, as the hypocrites do in the synagogues and in the streets, that they may be praised by men. Truly, I say to you, they have their reward. But when you give alms, do not let your left hand know what your right hand is doing, so that your alms may be in secret; and your Father who sees in secret will reward you. And when you pray, you must not be like the hypocrites; for they love to stand and pray in the synagogues and at the street corners, that they may be seen by men. Truly, I say to you, they have their reward. But when you pray, go into your room and shut the door and pray to your Father who is in secret; and your Father who sees in secret will reward you.'

Mt. 6:16-18 'And when you fast, do not look dismal, like the hypocrites, for they disfigure their faces that their fasting may be seen by men. Truly, I say to you, they have their reward. But when you fast, anoint your head and wash your face, that your fasting may not been seen by men but by your Father who is in secret; and your Father who sees in secret will reward you.'

Lk. 12:1 In the meantime, when so many thousands of the multitude had gathered together that they trod upon one another, he began to say to his disciples first, 'Beware of the leaven of the Pharisees, which is hypocrisy.'

Jn 10:12 'He who is a hireling and not a shepherd, whose own the sheep are not, sees the wolf coming and leaves the sheep and flees; and the wolf snatches them and scatters them.'

Lk. 11:39 And the Lord said to him, 'Now you Pharisees cleanse the outside of the cup and of the dish, but inside you are full of extortion and wickedness.'

Mt. 23:5-7 'They do all their deeds to be seen by men; for they make their phylacteries broad and their fringes long, and they love the place of honour at feasts and best seats in the synagogues and salutations in the market places, and being called rabbi by men.'

Mt. 12:13-15 'But woe to you, scribes and Pharisees, hypocrites! because you shut the Kingdom of heaven against men; for you neither enter yourselves, nor allow those who would enter to go in. Woe to you scribes and Pharisees, hypocrites! for you traverse sea and land to make a single proselyte, and when he becomes a proselyte, you make him twice as much a child of hell as yourselves.'

Mt. 23:25-28 'Woe to you, scribes and Pharisees, hypocrites! for you cleanse the outside of the cup and of the plate, but inside they are full of extortion and rapacity. You blind Pharisee! first cleanse the inside of the cup and of the plate, that the outside also may be clean.

Woe to you, scribes and Pharisees, hypocrites! for you are like white-washed tombs, which outwardly appear beautiful, but within they are full of dead men's bones and all uncleanness. So you also outwardly appear righteous to men, but within you are full of hypocrisy and iniquity.'

iii. Treachery, rejection

Jn 6:66-67	After this many of his disciples drew back and no longer went about with him, Jesus said to the twelve, 'Will you also go away?'
Jn 10:13	He flees because he is a hireling and cares nothing for the sheep.
Lk. 20:13,14	Then the owner of the vineyard said, 'What shall I do? I will send my beloved Son; it may be they will respect him'. But when the tenants saw him, they said to themselves, 'This is the heir; let us kill him, that the inheritance may be ours.'
Mt. 24:4,5	And Jesus answered them, 'Take heed that no one leads you astray. For many will come in my name, saying, "I am the Christ," and they will lead many astray.'
Mt. 13:12	'And brother will deliver up brother to death, and the father his child, and the children will rise against parents and have them put to death.'
Mt. 24:10	'And then many will fall away, and betray one another, and hate one another.'
Mk 13:21,22	'And then if any one says to you, "Look here is the Christ," or, "Look there he is," do not believe it. False Christs and false prophets will arise and show signs and wanders, to lead astray, if possible, the elect.'
Lk. 22:3-6	Then Satan entered into Judas called Iscariot, who was of the number of the twelve; he went away and conferred with the chief priests and captains how he might betray him to them. And they were glad and engaged to give him money. So he agreed, and sought an opportunity to betray him to them in the absence of the multitude.
Jn 13:2	And during supper, when the devil had already put it into the heart of Judas Iscariot, Simon's son, to betray him....
Jn 13:18	'I am not speaking of you all; I know whom I have chosen; it is that the Scripture may be fulfilled, "He who ate my bread has lifted his heel against me."'
Jn 13:21	When Jesus had thus spoken, he was troubled in spirit, and testified, 'Truly, truly, I say to you, one of you will betray me.'

Jn 13:27	Then after the morsel, Satan entered into him. Jesus said to him, 'What you are going to do, do quickly.'
Mt. 26:48-50	Now the betrayer had given them a sign, saying, 'The one I shall kiss is the man; seize him.' And he came up to Jesus at once and said, 'Hail master.' And he kissed him. Jesus said to him, 'Friend, why are you here?' Then they came up and laid hands on Jesus and seized him.
Lk. 22:60-62	But Peter said, 'Man, I do not know what you are saying.' And immediately, while he was still speaking, the cock crowed, and the Lord turned and looked at Peter. And Peter remembered the word of the Lord, how he had said to him, 'Before the cock crows today, you will deny me three times.' And he wept bitterly.

see also: 10.i. Lack of Faith is blameworthy
11.v. Unanswered calls
17.viii. Disobedience

19. Evangelizing: I

i. Advice on evangelizing

Jn 4:35-38	'. . . Do you not say, "There are yet four months, then comes the harvest"? I tell you, lift up your eyes, and see how the fields are already white for harvest. He who reaps receives wages, and gathers fruit for eternal life, so that sower and reaper may rejoice together. For here the saying holds true, "One sows and another reaps." I sent you to reap that for which you did not labour; others have laboured, and you have entered into their labour.'
Mk 1:38	And he said to them, 'Let us go on to the next towns, that I may preach there also; for that is why I came out.'
Mk 3:14	And he appointed twelve, to be with him, and to be sent out to preach and have authority to cast out demons.
Mt. 7:6	'Do not give dogs what is holy; and do not throw your pearls before swine, lest they trample them under foot and turn to attack you.'
Mt. 12:36,37	'. . . I tell you, on the day of judgment men will render account for every careless word they utter; for by your words you will be justified, and by your words you will be condemned.'
Mk 4:21-23	And he said to them, 'Is a lamp brought in to be put under a bushel, or under a bed, and not on a stand? For there is nothing hid, except to be made manifest; nor is anything secret, except to come to light. If any man has ears to hear, let him hear.'
Mt. 13:51,52	'Have you understood all this?' They said to him, 'Yes.' And he said to them, 'Therefore every scribe who has been trained for the kingdom of heaven is like a householder who brings out of his treasure what is new and what is old.'
Lk. 8:38,39	The man from whom the demons had gone begged that he might be with him; but he sent him away, saying, 'Return to your home and declare how much God has done for you.'

Mk 6:12,13 So they went out and preached that men should repent. And they cast out many demons, and anointed with oil many that were sick and healed them.

Mk 6:30,31 The apostles returned to Jesus, and told him all that they had done and taught. And he said to them, 'Come away by yourselves to a lonely place, and rest a while.'

Mt. 5:13 'You are the salt of the earth; but if salt has lost its taste, how shall its saltness be restored? It is no longer good for anything except to be thrown out and trodden under foot by men.'

Jn 10:16 '. . . and I have other sheep, that are not of this fold; I must bring them also, and they will heed my voice. So there shall be one flock, one shepherd.'

Lk. 10:1-20 After this the Lord appointed seventy others, and sent them on ahead of him, two by two, into every town and place where he himself was about to come. And he said to them, 'The harvest is plentiful, but the labourers are few; pray therefore the Lord of the harvest to send out labourers into his harvest. Go your way; behold, I send you out as lambs in the midst of wolves. Carry no purse, no bag, no sandals; and salute no one on the road. Whatever house you enter, first say, "Peace be to this house." And if a son of peace is there, your peace shall rest upon him; but if not, it shall return to you. And remain in the same house, eating and drinking what they provide, for the labourer deserves his wages; do not go from house to house. Whenever you enter a town and they receive you, eat what is set before you; heal the sick in it and say to them, "The kingdom of God has come near to you." But whenever you enter a town and they do not receive you, go into its streets and say, "Even the dust of your town that clings to our feet, we wipe off against you; nevertheless know this, that the kingdom of God has come near." I tell you, it shall be more tolerable on that day for Sodom than for that town.

'Woe to you, Chorazin! woe to you, Bethsaida! for if the mighty works done in you had been done in Tyre and Sidon, they would have repented long ago, sitting in sackcloth and ashes. But it shall be more tolerable in the judgment for Tyre and Sidon than for you. And you, Capernaum, will you be exalted to heaven? You shall be brought down to Hades.

'He who hears you hears me, and he who rejects you rejects me, and he who rejects me rejects him who sent me.'

The seventy returned with joy, saying, 'Lord, even the demons are subject to us in your name.' And he said to them, 'I saw Satan fall like lightning from heaven. Behold, I have given you authority to tread upon serpents and scorpions, and over all the power of the enemy; and nothing shall hurt you. Nevertheless do not rejoice in this, that the spirits are subject to you; but rejoice that your names are written in heaven.'

Mt. 5:14-16

'You are the light of the world. A city set on a hill cannot be hid. Nor do men light a lamp and put it under a bushel, but on a stand, and it gives light to all in the house. Let your light so shine before men, that they may see your good works and give glory to your Father who is in heaven.'

Lk. 12:1-3

In the meantime, when so many thousands of the multitude had gathered together that they trod upon one another, he began to say to his disciples first, 'Beware of the leaven of the Pharisees, which is hypocrisy. Nothing is covered up that will not be revealed, or hidden that will not be known. Whatever you have said in the dark shall be heard in the light, and what you have whispered in private rooms shall be proclaimed upon the housetops.'

Mt. 10:24-26

'A disciple is not above his teacher, nor a servant above his master; it is enough for the disciple to be like his teacher, and the servant like his master. If they have called the master of the house Beelzebul, how much more will they malign those of his household. So have no fear of them; for nothing is covered that will not be revealed, or hidden that will not be known.'

Mt. 10:19-20

'. . . When they deliver you up, do not be anxious how you are to speak or what you are to say; for what you are to say will be given to you in that hour; for it is not you who speak, but the Spirit of your Father speaking through you.'

Lk. 12:49,50 'I come to cast fire upon the earth; and would that it were already kindled! I have a baptism to be baptized with; and how I am constrained until it is accomplished!'

Lk. 13:6-9 And he told this parable: 'A man had a fig tree planted in his vineyard; and he came seeking fruit on it and found none. And he said to the vinedresser, "Lo, these three years I have come seeking fruit on this fig tree, and I find none. Cut it down; why should it use up the ground?" And he answered him, "Let it alone, sir, this year also, till I dig about it and put on manure. And if it bears fruit next year, well and good; but if not, you can cut it down."'

Lk. 14:23,24 '... And the master said to the servant, "Go out to the highways and hedges, and compel people to come in, that my house may be filled. For I tell you, none of those men who were invited shall taste my banquet."'

Jn 11:7-9 Then after this he said to the disciples, 'Let us go into Judea again.' The disciples said to him, 'Rabbi, the Jews were but now seeking to stone you, and are you going there again?' Jesus answered, 'Are there not twelve hours in the day? If any one walks in the day, he does not stumble, because he sees the light of this world.'

Jn 11:53,54 So from that day on they took counsel how to put him to death. Jesus therefore no longer went about openly among the Jews, but went from there to the country near the wilderness, to a town called Ephraim; and there he stayed with the disciples.

Lk. 22:35,36 And he said to them, 'When I sent you out with no purse or bag or sandals, did you lack anything?' They said, 'Nothing'. He said to them, 'But now, let him who has a purse take it, and likewise a bag. And let him who has no sword sell his mantle and buy one.'

Lk. 24:46-49 ... and said to them, 'Thus it is written, that the Christ should suffer and on the third day rise from the dead, and that repentance and forgiveness of sins should be preached in his name to all nations, beginning from

Jerusalem. You are witnesses of these things. And behold, I send the promise of my Father upon you; but stay in the city, until you are clothed with power from on high.'

ii. Keeping the Message secret

Mk 3:11,12 — And whenever the unclean spirits beheld him, they fell down before him and cried out, 'You are the Son of God.' And he strictly ordered them not to make him known.

Mt. 12:15,16 — Jesus, aware of this, withdrew from there. And many followed him, and he healed them all, and ordered them not to make him known.

Mt. 13:13 — '... This is why I speak to them in parables, because seeing they do not see, and hearing they do not hear, nor do they understand.'

Mt. 13:34,35 — All this Jesus said to the crowds in parables; indeed he said nothing to them without a parable. This was to fulfil what was spoken by the prophet:
'I will open my mouth in parables,
I will utter what has been hidden since the foundation of the world.'

Mk 4:33,34 — With many such parables he spoke the word to them, as they were able to hear it; he did not speak to them without a parable, but privately to his own disciples he explained everything.

Mk 5:43 — And he strictly charged them that no one should know this, and told them to give her something to eat.

Jn 6:15 — Perceiving then that they were about to come and take him by force to make him king, Jesus withdrew again to the hills by himself.

Jn 7:1 — After this Jesus went about in Galilee; he would not go about in Judea, because the Jews sought to kill him.

Mt. 10:5,6 — These twelve Jesus sent out, charging them, 'Go nowhere among the Gentiles, and enter no town of the Samaritans, but go rather to the lost sheep of the house of Israel.'

Mt. 15:24	He answered, 'I was sent only to the lost sheep of the house of Israel.'
Mk 7:36	And he charged them to tell no one, but the more he charged them, the more zealously they proclaimed it.
Mk 8:26	And he sent him away to his home saying, 'Do not even enter the village.'
Mt. 16:20	Then he strictly charged the disciples to tell no one that he was the Christ.
Mt. 17:9	And as they were coming down the mountain, Jesus commanded them, 'Tell no one the vision, until the Son of man is raised from the dead.'
Mk 9:29-31	And he said to them, 'This kind cannot be driven out by anything but prayer and fasting.' They went on from there and passed through Galilee. And he would not have any one know it; for he was teaching his disciples, saying to them, 'The Son of man will be delivered into the hands of men, and they will kill him; and when he is killed, after three days he will rise.'
Jn 7:3-6	So his brethren said to him, 'Leave here and go to Judea, that your disciples may see the works you are doing. For no man works in secret if he seeks to be known openly. If you do these things, show yourself to the world.' For even his brethren did not believe in him. Jesus said to them, 'My time has not yet come, but your time is always here.'
Mt. 9:30	And their eyes were opened. And Jesus sternly charged them, 'See that no one knows it.'

See also: 11.iii. Commissions to members of the Twelve
11.iv. Other commissions or calls

20. Evangelizing: II

i. Christ preaches

Mt. 4:17 — From that time Jesus began to preach, saying, 'Repent, for the kingdom of heaven is at hand.'

Lk. 4:16-21 — And he came to Nazareth, where he had been brought up; and he went to the synagogue, as his custom was, on the sabbath day. And he stood up to read; and there was given to him the book of the prophet Isaiah. He opened the book and found the place where it was written,
'The Spirit of the Lord is upon me,
because he has anointed me to preach good news to the poor.
He has sent me to proclaim release to the captives
and recovering of sight to the blind,
to set at liberty those who are oppressed,
to proclaim the acceptable year of the Lord.'
And he closed the book, and gave it back to the attendant, and sat down; and the eyes of all in the synagogue were fixed on him. And he began to say to them, 'Today this scripture has been fulfilled in your hearing.'

Mk 1:21,22 — And they went into Capernaum; and immediately on the sabbath he entered the synagogue and taught. And they were astonished at his teaching, for he taught them as one who had authority, and not as the scribes.

Mk 1:38,39 — And he said to them. 'Let us go on to the next towns, that I may preach there also; for that is why I came out.' And he went throughout all Galilee, preaching in their synagogues and casting out demons.

Lk. 5:3 — Getting into one of the boats, which was Simon's, he asked him to put out a little from the land. And he sat down and taught the people from the boat.

Mt. 5:1-3 — Seeing the crowds, he went up on the mountain, and when he sat down his disciples came to him. And he opened his mouth and taught them, saying, 'Blessed are the poor in spirit, for theirs is the kingdom of heaven.'

Lk. 8:1-3 — Soon afterwards he went on through cities and villages, preaching and bringing the good news of the kingdom of God. And the twelve were with him, and also some women who had been healed of evil spirits and infirmities: Mary, called Magdalene, from whom seven demons had gone out, and Joanna, the wife of Chuza, Herod's steward, and Susanna, and many others, who provided for them out of their means.

Mk 4:1 — Again he began to teach beside the sea. And a very large crowd gathered about him, so that he got into a boat and sat in it on the sea; and the whole crowd was beside the sea on the land.

Mt. 13:34,35 — All this Jesus said to the crowds in parables; indeed he said nothing to them without a parable. This was to fulfil what was spoken by the prophet: 'I will open my mouth in parables. I will utter what has been hidden since the foundation of the world.'

Mk 4:33,34 — With many such parables he spoke the word to them, as they were able to hear it; he did not speak to them without a parable, but privately to his own disciples he explained everything.

Mt. 13:54 — . . . and coming to his own country he taught them in their own synagogue, so that they were astonished, and said, 'Where did this man get this wisdom and these mighty works?'

Mt. 9:35 — And Jesus went about all the cities and villages, teaching in their synagogues and preaching the gospel of the kingdom, and healing every disease and every infirmity.

Jn 6:60,61 — Many of his disciples, when they heard it, said, 'This is a hard saying; who can listen to it?' But Jesus, knowing in himself that his disciples murmured at it, said to them, 'Do you take offence at this?'

Mt. 11:20 — Then he began to upbraid the cities where most of his mighty works had been done, because they did not repent.

Jn 7:26 — 'And here he is, speaking openly, and they say nothing to him! Can it be that the authorities really know that this is the Christ?'

Jn 7:37 — On the last day of the feast, the great day, Jesus stood up and proclaimed, 'If anyone thirst, let him come to me and drink.'

Jn 8:2 — Early in the morning he came again to the temple; all the people came to him, and he sat down and taught them.

Mk 10:1 — And he left there and went to the region of Judea and beyond the Jordan, and crowds gathered to him again; and again, as his custom was, he taught them.

Lk. 14:25,26 — Now great multitudes accompanied him; and he turned and said to them, 'If any one comes to me and does not hate his own father and mother and wife and children and brothers and sisters, yes, and even his own life, he cannot be my disciple.'

Mt. 21:23 — And when he entered the temple, the chief priests and the elders of the people came up to him as he was teaching, and said, 'By what authority are you doing these things, and who gave you this authority?'

Lk. 21:37,38 — And every day he was teaching in the temple, but at night he went out and lodged on the mount called Olivet. And early in the morning all the people came to him in the temple to hear him.

ii. Christ's reputation spreads

Lk. 4:14 — And Jesus returned in the power of the Spirit into Galilee, and a report concerning him went out through all the surrounding country.

Lk. 4:22 — And all spoke well of him, and wondered at the gracious words which proceeded out of his mouth; and they said, 'Is not this Joseph's son?'

Mk 1:28 — And at once his fame spread everywhere throughout all the surrounding region of Galilee.

Mk 1:45 — But he went out and began to talk freely about it, and to spread the news, so that Jesus could no longer openly enter a town, but was out in the country; and people came to him from every quarter.

Mt. 4:24 — So his fame spread throughout all Syria, and they brought him all the sick, those afflicted with various diseases and pains, demoniacs, epileptics, and paralytics, and he healed them.

Lk. 7:17 — And this report concerning him spread through the whole of Judea and all the surrounding country.

Mk 5:14,15	The herdsmen fled, and told it in the city and in the country. And people came to see what it was that had happened. And they came to Jesus, and saw the demoniac sitting there, clothed and in his right mind, the man who had had the legion; and they were afraid.
Mt. 9:26	And the report of this went through all that district.
Mk 7:36	And he charged them to tell no one; but the more he charged them, the more zealously they proclaimed it.
Mt. 9:30,31	And their eyes were opened. And Jesus sternly charged them, 'See that no one knows it.' But they went away and spread his fame through all that district.
Lk. 11:14	Now he was casting out a demon that was dumb; when the demon had gone out, the dumb man spoke, and the people marvelled.
Jn 12:9	When the great crows of the Jews learned that he was there, they came, not only on account of Jesus but also to see Lazarus, whom he had raised from the dead.
Jn 12:17-19	The crowd that had been with him when he called Lazarus out of the tomb and raised him from the dead bore witness. The reason why the crowd went to meet him was that they heard he had done this sign. The pharisees then said to one another, 'You see that you can do nothing; look, the world has gone after him.'

iii. Spontaneous witnesses

Jn 4:28,29	So the woman left her water jar, and went away into the city, and said to the people, 'Come, see a man who told me all that I ever did. Can this be the Christ?'
Mk 1:45	But he went out and began to talk freely about it, and to spread the news, so that Jesus could no longer openly enter a town, but was out in the country; and people came to him from every quarter.
Jn 5:15	The man went away and told the Jews that it was Jesus who had healed him.
Mk 9:38-39	John said to him, 'Teacher, we saw a man casting out demons in your name, and we forbade him, because he

was not following us.' But Jesus said, 'Do not forbid him; for no one who does a mighty work in my name will be able soon after to speak evil of me.'

Jn 9:10,11 They said to him, 'Then how were your eyes opened?' He answered, 'The man called Jesus made clay and anointed my eyes and said to me, "Go to Siloam and wash," so I went and washed and received my sight.'

Lk. 19:8,10 And Zaccheus stood and said to the Lord, 'Behold, Lord, the half of my goods I give to the poor; and if I have defrauded any one of anything, I restore it fourfold.' Jesus said to him, 'Today salvation has come to this house, since he also is a son of Abraham. For the Son of man came to seek and to save the lost.'

Jn 12:12-15 The next day a great crowd who had come to the feast heard that Jesus was coming to Jerusalem. So they took branches of palm trees and went out to meet him, crying, 'Hosanna! Blessed is he who comes in the name of the Lord, even the King of Israel!' And Jesus found a young ass and sat upon it; as it is written,

'Fear not, daughter of Zion;
behold your king is coming,
sitting on an ass's colt!'

Jn 12:49-53 'For I have not spoken on my own authority; the Father who sent me has himself given me commandment what to say and what to speak. And I know that his commandment is eternal life. What I say, therefore, I say as the Father has bidden me.'

Mt. 27:54 When the centurion and those who were with him, keeping watch over Jesus, saw the earthquake and what took place, they were filled with awe, and said, 'Truly this was the Son of God!'

Appendix for Retreatants

Suggested plan for the use of 'The Gospels for Prayer' in conjunction with the Spiritual Exercises of St Ignatius Loyola.

For the Exercises on:	*Consult:*
Prayer	1.
The Fundamental Principle	3.ii, 4, 13.i, 13.ii.
First week	2, 3, 9.iii, 10.i, 15.v, 15.vi, 16.ii, 17.viii, 18.
Call of the King	9.i, 14.i, 15.i-iv.
Second week	2, 3.i, 3.ii, 9, 10, 14, 15.
Third week	5.iii, 6.i, 9.iii.
Fourth week	4, 5.iv.
Contemplation for obtaining love	4, 7, 9.i, 10.iv, 13.i, 13.ii.
Discernment	3.i, 3.ii, 9, 10, 14.
Alms	12.
Scruples	3.i, 3.ii, 9, 10, 14.
Thinking with the Church	2.iii, 17.